Eggs: Facts and Fancies About Them

by Anna Barrows

with an introduction by Jackson Chambers

This work contains material that was originally published in 1890.

This publication is within the Public Domain.

*This edition is reprinted for educational purposes
and in accordance with all applicable Federal Laws.*

COVER CREDITS

Front Cover
by Omrihayu (Own work)
[CC BY-SA 4.0 (https://creativecommons.org/licenses/by-sa/4.0)],
via Wikimedia Commons

Back Cover
American Robin Eggs in Nest by Laslovarga (Own work)
[CC BY-SA 3.0 (https://creativecommons.org/licenses/by-sa/3.0)],
via Wikimedia Commons

Research / Sources
Wikimedia Commons
www.Commons.Wikimedia.org

Many thanks to all the incredible photographers, artists,
researchers, and archivists who share their great work.

PLEASE NOTE :
As with all reprinted books of this age that are intended to perfectly reproduce the original edition, considerable pains and effort had to be undertaken to correct fading and sometimes outright damage to existing proofs of this title. At times, this task can be quite monumental, requiring an almost total rebuilding of some pages from digital proofs of multiple copies. Despite this, imperfections still sometimes exist in the final proof and may detract slightly from the visual appearance of the text.

DISCLAIMER :
Due to the age of this book, some methods or practices may have been deemed unsafe or unacceptable in the interim years. In utilizing the information herein, you do so at your own risk. We republish antiquarian books without judgment or revisionism, solely for their historical and cultural importance, and for educational purposes.

Self Reliance Books

Get more historic titles on animal and stock breeding, gardening and old fashioned skills by visiting us at:

http://selfreliancebooks.blogspot.com/

INTRODUCTION

I am very pleased to bring you this unusual, unique old book - ***Eggs : Facts and Fancies About Them***. It was written in 1890, more than 120 years ago, by Anna Barrows.

This was a wonderful find! I love to discover unusual and strange old books to republish – books that probably haven't been laid eyes on in a century or more. And this one is a most unusual find indeed!

The book follows the history and the mythos of the humble egg. Inside you will find *facts* and figures on everything from *The Chemistry of the Egg, Tests of the Freshness of Eggs, Medicine, Commercial Statistics and Eggs as Food*, to *fancies* like *Mythology* and *Superstitions*, and chapters such as *Eggs in Literature, Easter, Romances in Eggs, Eggs in China*, and more.

Eggs : Facts and Fancies About Them is a gem of a find that would make a unique, thoughtful gift for anybody interested in history, mythology or the origins of things.

Jackson Chambers,

State of Jefferson, November 2017

GAME BANTAMS.

(Specially drawn to illustrate Mr. Proud's articles on Bantams.)

BLACK ROSECOMB.

JAPANESE.

SILVER AND GOLDEN SEBRIGHTS.
BANTAMS.
BRAHMAS.

WHITE ROSECOMB.

BOOTED.

PREFACE.

THIS book has been compiled with a twofold object: to increase the use of eggs as food, and thus increase their production.

No other article of food is suitable alike for old and young, for rich and poor, for epicures and ascetics, for athletes and invalids.

Believing that a greater use of eggs as food can best be brought about by a knowledge of their composition and the principles of cookery, the compiler has, by careful classification, tried to diminish rather than to multiply recipes and yet present such variations that any housekeeper may adapt each method to the materials already at hand.

Few employments are better suited to women with small capital, either of money or physical strength, than the raising of eggs for market.

The preparation of eggs for food, especially in cakes and desserts, is also a remunerative business for women.

Small flocks of poultry are usually more successful than large ones.

This work can be carried on at home, and proves a great economy of the household waste.

"Out of bugs and worms and seeds, and what it can pick and scratch from the waste of Nature's laboratory, the hen produces the fair white egg — one of the most delicious morsels to the human palate, one which fills the heart of man with loving-kindness."

In the words of a writer two hundred and fifty years ago:

"Believe, dear friend, that no alchemist ever produced from furnace or alembic, so rare a treasure as you may obtain from your hens, if you only know how to combine labor and delight."

PREFACE.

Among the books examined in the arrangement of this little work are encyclopædias, general and specific, chemistry and other books relating to foods, as well as a large number of cook books. The most helpful, however, have been "The Chemistry of Cooking," by W. M. Williams, "Foods," by Edward Smith, M. D., "The Franco-American Cookery Book," "The Modern Householder," by T. J. Murrey, "How to Cook and Serve Eggs," by G. Hill, [published in England in 1867], "All About Eggs" [published in Chicago by Victor Palmer], and books on cookery by Mrs. Lincoln, Miss Corson, Miss Parloa, Marion Harland, Helen Campbell and others.

EGGS

NAME AND SHAPE.

THE egg is one of the few things in the world original and positive in itself. Though some specimens are round and some oblong, the usual shape cannot be described by words applicable to other objects.

The egg is *oval;* that is, egg-shaped, since that word is derived directly from the Latin name for the egg — *ovum.*

Not only does the egg name itself, but it gives rise to words descriptive of other objects.

Ovum may have been derived from the Latin *avis,* a bird. From this root come the words oval, ovary, ovate, ovolo, ovule, etc.

The Greek word meaning egg was ᾠόν; and from this comes oölogy, etc. The same word was sometimes used to describe a bald head.

Tennyson uses the simile, " bald as an egg."

From the Anglo-Saxon *oeg* comes the word we use to-day.   Chaucer and other early writers use the forms *ey*, *eg*, egge.

The verb to egg, meaning to incite, is now nearly obsolete.

" Thou should'st be prancing on thy steed
To egg thy soldiers forward in thy wars."

The egg and dart, egg and tongue, egg and anchor, are ornaments for the ovolo molding in architecture.

Egg-shell china is so-called from its extreme delicacy.   The egg-plant is named from the shape of its fruit.

Nest eggs and bad eggs are phrases often used metaphorically.

The size of the egg has long been a standard of measure, and its specific gravity a test for solutions.

The first watches were egg-shaped, and, from their origin in that city, were called Nuremberg animated eggs.

The new *Century* dictionary gives more than fifty derivations and compounds of the word egg.

" Nature is very skillful; we don't take half as many hints from her as we might. Do you observe these eggs all of one color — those delicate blues — these exquisite drabs? If you ever wish to paint a room, take one of these eggs for a model, and you will arrive at such tints as no painter ever imagined out of his own head, I know."

CHAS. READE.

The nine thousand varieties of known birds furnish every shade of color in eggs. This is a device of Nature for their protection. Birds whose nests are covered lay white eggs, while in open nests in fields or on the sand the eggs are colored like surrounding objects.

The surface of the shell may be rough or

smooth as if polished. Eggs of some sea-birds are covered with a glutinous substance to prevent their slipping off the sand or rocks.

" On few things have so much beauty been lavished. Just peep in any lane or brake, in spring, into a bird's nest, and lying cosily in their mossy couch you will behold a number of mysterious spheres, every one of them with life within, but externally smooth and brilliant as a gem, penciled with delicate lines, flecked with lapis lazuli or ruby, clouded, streaked, furnished with thousands of invisible pores, through which the air penetrates to the imprisoned bird, to hasten its development and co-operate with animal heat in imparting to it all the mysterious powers of organization and vitality."

" Considering one of these marvels from our view we should think it something to last forever, while it is only for a few days.

Pierce the shell and we find a matrix white, thin and delicate as the petals of a flower, to protect it from the shell.

Then follows the mighty process of matter quickening into life, the metamorphosis of these fluids into bones, flesh, feathers, talons, heart and brain with the machinery of voice, instinct, affection, emotion, whether in the ostrich or the humming-bird no larger than a pea."

Chamber's Journal.

MYTHOLOGY.

EW articles of common life have figured as largely in history and fable
as the egg.

The proverb " *Omne Vivum ex Ovo*," is the basis of the religious belief of many Eastern nations.

The formation of the world from chaos was well compared to the development of the chicken from the egg.

The mundane or universal egg may be traced in all mythology. Under various forms the same legend appears, namely: that on the waste of waters a mighty bird deposited an egg from which the earth was evolved.

In his " Histoire Religieuse du Calendrier " [Paris, 1776], the learned M. Court de Gebelin gives many of these legends.

Here it is only possible to give a condensed translation from this quaint old French book.

"In the philosophy and theology of the Egyptians, Persians, Gauls, Greeks and Romans the egg was the emblem of the universe, the work of the Supreme Deity.

The Egyptian divinity, Kneph or Emeph — a word in their language meaning good or benevolent — is painted in the human form to indicate his intelligence; androgynous, to signify his absolute independence, having on his head a butterfly to designate his activity, and with an egg issuing from his mouth to prove his fertility.

From the egg proceeded Phthah, or the Fire, from whom the Greeks derive their Vulcan. To this divinity was addressed the famous inscription on the Temple of Sais, ending with these words —

'The fruit which I have produced is the Sun.'

According to Orpheus, who carried this doctrine into Greece, there first existed the immense, eternal chaos from which all things were to be produced.

It was neither light nor shade, damp nor dry, warm nor cold, but all together — and had the form of an immense egg.

It was the origin of all things, and began by the separation of the four elements, from two of which the heavens are formed and from the others the earth, and by the participation of these all beings are born.

The spirit of God brooded upon the waters as the hen upon her egg.

This egg becomes the base of a multitude of allegories revolting and absurd when they do not approach their model, but very ingenious when in the same key. Among these are the fables of the birth of Hercules; the sons of Jove born from an egg — Castor and Pollux; Venus born from the bosom of the waters; Semiramis born from an egg cast up by the waters — and others."

The Persians believed in two deities; one born of light, the other of shade, who made war upon each other.

The first produced twenty-four good spirits inclosed in an egg, which was invaded by evil spirits proceeding from the other, and since that time good and evil have been mingled on earth. The Hindoos held the egg to be the source of all things, and therefore refrained from eating it.

The Mongolian races have a tradition that a mystic bird laid an egg on the bosom of one of their deities, there to be hatched. He let it fall into the water and it broke; the upper part then became the sky, the lower the earth; the liquid white formed the sun, the yolk the moon, and fragments of the shell became stars.

The Egyptians saw in the egg an emblem of the restoration of mankind after the deluge, and venerated it accordingly. It often appears in their hieroglyphics.

The egg and tongue of architecture is thought to be a relic of the head of Isis, representing a necklace of the mundane egg, and the tongue of the serpent of immortality.

The Jews found in the egg a symbol of bondage and wonderful deliverance, and used it as a type of their departure from Egypt, and it appeared on the Passover table.

The modern Hebrews still use eggs at the Passover season, as an emblem of the rolling fate of Israel.

The peculiar shape of the dome of the Mohammedan mosques is regarded as a vestige of the early egg worship.

Egg-shaped stones have been excavated in the ruins of many cities of the East.

The Greeks and Romans adopted these theories from the earlier nations.

At one time in Greece, philosophers tried to keep people from eating eggs, since they contained all the elements of life. The shell represented the earth; the white, water; the yolk, fire; air was found under the shell, and the germ of life it was a sin to destroy.

Among the Romans eggs were used in the holy ceremonies of Bacchus, and in rites of expiation. Juvenal informs us that at the autumn equinox, to escape the ravages of that season, an offering of one hundred eggs was made.

The worship of the egg gradually degenerated into the ceremonies of magicians, and the use of the egg, even at the present day, among ignorant people, in various love charms and divinations, can thus be traced back to the mundane egg.

SUPERSTITIONS.

"There's something strange about egg shells,
That makes them proof against all spells."

TUDOR JENKS.

EGGS, and especially their shells, have been thought potent aids in witch-craft.

Irish and English nurses once instructed children to push their spoons through the shell of an egg, after eating its contents, " to keep the witches from making a boat of it."

These lines from Beaumont and Fletcher show the common belief:

" The devil should think of purchasing that egg-shell,
To victual out a wife for the Bermoothus."

(*i. e.* Bermudas.)

Sir Thomas Browne tells us another reason for breaking the shells, lest the witches should draw or prick their names therein and thus injure the person who had partaken of the egg.

Eggs laid on holy days were supposed to possess helpful qualities against all ills.

In 1584, Reginald Scot says, " To hang an egg, laid on Ascension Day, in the roof of a house preserveth the same from all hurts."

Eggs produced on Good Friday were also kept, since they had power to extinguish any fire on which they might be thrown.

The Netherlanders say that ague may be kept at a distance by eating on Easter Day two eggs laid on Good Friday. While in North Germany the shells are broken after the contents are eaten to keep away the same dread visitor.

Dreaming of eggs is a prediction of trouble, though if the shells be broken when they appear the danger is averted.

Scotch fishermen think it unlucky to have eggs on board their boats, as they will bring contrary winds.

In many parts of England eggs are not allowed to leave the house after sunset, for fear of ill luck, and to have them brought in would be equally disastrous.

On Halloween, if the white of egg be dropped into any pure liquid, the shape it takes will indicate the future of the person trying the charm.

A maiden anxious to see her future husband, spends the day of St. Agnes in silence and fasting, then takes the yolk from a hard-boiled egg, fills the cavity with salt and eats shell and all. After sundry incantations she may then count on seeing the desired one in her dreams.

Hebrew mourners returning from the funeral sometimes partake of a hard-boiled egg, sprinkled with ashes instead of salt. Probably this has reference to the resurrection.

EASTER.

SIDE from their use as food eggs are connected with one of the great festivals of the Christian church.

From the earliest ages, all nations have celebrated the awakening of nature at the vernal equinox, and the day we know as Easter may be considered a combination of these festivities with the Jewish Passover, but given a new significance by the risen Christ.

The early church was divided on the question of the proper time for the observance of the resurrection, and the matter was not decided until A. D. 325 at the Nicene Council. The settlement of the controversy was one of the questions which led Constantine to call the council: "That everywhere the great feast of Easter should be observed upon one and the same day, and that not the day, of the Jewish Passover, but as had been generally observed, upon the Sunday afterward."

The date may be as early as March 22, or as late as April 25. It is the first Sunday following the full moon, which appears on or after March 21.

The word Easter may have been derived from the same root as east, and applied to this season of the year which was proverbially angry and stormy.* Another probable source of the word is Ostara or Eoestre, the name of an Anglo-Saxon goddess — corresponding to the Latin Aurora — whose festival occurred at this season.

The Saxons when converted to Christianity continued many of their customs at the spring festival — but instead of saying " Eoestre hath awakened," greeted each other with " The Lord hath risen."

Until within a comparatively short time special services and observance of Easter were confined to the Catholic and Greek churches;

* Oster-monat, or month of the east wind, was the Saxon name for April.

now the festival is generally celebrated. An
increase in the symbolic gifts at this season may
be noticed, and many old customs are revived.

The most prevalent and characteristic custom
of the Easter festival has always been the giving
of eggs. Sometimes they were eaten, oftener
kept as amulets, or used in playing games.

The pagan people at their new year feasts
presented each other with eggs as a type of the
new life of nature — which they colored to show
their joy at the return of spring.

Barbarous nations in Africa and South
America offer eggs to their idols at the spring
festivals. The Greeks had the custom of pre-
senting colored eggs. The Romans celebrated
the new year with egg games in honor of Castor
and Pollux.

The Druids used eggs in the worship of the
goddess Eoestre.

What wonder that with all the traditions
and superstitions connected with the egg, that
this custom was continued even had it not been
an appropriate emblem of the resurrection?

The early Christians continued this practice and colored the eggs red to symbolize the blood of their redemption.

St. Augustine recognized the egg as a type of hope. Marble eggs have been found in the tombs of saints and martyrs.

The contrast between the cold, lifeless egg and the warm downy chicken full of life and motion, may well have made the former an emblem of the endless life of the soul.

A German writer says :

" The egg as a symbol of the resurrection of Jesus, who broke forth from the grave as a chicken from the shell, has been from very ancient date an Easter gift with Christians."

After the fourth century the Church prohibited the use of eggs as well as of other animal food during Lent, but the hens were heretical enough to keep on laying and the accumulated eggs were dyed for children at Easter.

The Greek Church still forbids the use of eggs during Lent, but other churches allow their use during the Lenten fast.

Eggs were long regarded as the transition food at the beginning and end of Lent.

" And hence the egg feast formerly at Oxford when the scholars took leave of that kind of food on the Saturday after Ash Wednesday."
Brand's Antiquities.

" By the common people too, the preceding Saturday (before the first Sunday in Lent) in Oxfordshire particularly is called Egg Saturday."
Hampson Medii Aevi Kalendrier.

It is supposed that the custom of decorating eggs at Easter arose among Catholics from joy at returning to their favorite food.

According to an old tradition, the bells went to Rome to be blessed at Easter time, and the eggs were dyed scarlet like the cardinal's cloak, to show that the bells had brought them back from Rome. Angels, too, were believed to descend with baskets of eggs for the faithful, and sometimes an evil egg found its way with the others with dire results.

1605 – 1621.

In the ritual of Pope Paul V., made for the use of England, Ireland and Scotland, occurs this benediction :

"Bless, O Lord, we beseech thee, this thy creature of EGGS, that it may become a wholesome sustenance to thy faithful servants, eating it in thankfulness to thee, on account of the Resurrection of our Lord Jesus Christ."

It had been the custom of the pagan priest to bless offerings of eggs. The line " Creepinge to the cross with egges and apples," shows that Christians continued the custom.

A sermon preached in England in 1570 mentions that certain ones on Good Friday " offered unto Christe Egges and Bacon to be in his favor till Easter Day was past."

An entry among the household expenses of Edward I. of England, of eighteen pence for four hundred eggs for Easter, shows the observance of the custom at that period and the extreme cheapness of **eggs.**

In certain parts of England eggs rose in price at this time.

It was once customary in Scotland to search for wild fowl's eggs on Easter morning for good luck.

"Here are two or three jolly boys all of one
        mind;
We've come a pace-egging and hope you'll be
        kind;
We hope you'll be kind with your eggs and
        your beer,
And we'll come no more near you until the
        New Year."

Easter is to the Russians what Christmas is to the Germans. It is the day of all the year for family gatherings, and is if possible celebrated in new garments.

The people offer each other eggs, saying Christ is risen.

At St. Petersburg hundreds come to kiss the hand of the empress, who rewards each one with a decorated egg of porcelain.

Early in the morning the churches are full for the mass, while all around are servants with dishes of eggs, waiting to have them blessed.

In Poland Lent is rigidly observed, and at its close animal food is partaken of with great solemnity.

The table is laid to represent a fort. Pyramids of cold hard-boiled eggs surrounded by coils of sausage are the ordnance stores.

The host begins the feast by cutting one of the eggs in thin slices and shares a slice with each guest in turn, while offering congratulations of the day.

This ceremony is performed in turn by every one with all the others present.

In France hens' nests were formerly ransacked for the largest eggs for an Easter tribute to the king. The priests used to go from house to house, leaving their blessings and receiving eggs enough to last for many weeks.

During the reigns of Louis XIV. and XV. after mass on Easter Sunday it was the custom for the king to distribute gilded eggs to his courtiers.

Passion week in Paris may be called the feast of eggs. In the streets may be heard the cries of " des œufs " from women bearing piles of red and white eggs on barrows, and everybody presents his neighbor with an egg real or artificial.

Easter eggs are usually boiled hard, the shells being stained with bright colors and variously decorated.

Boiling in dye gives any desired color to the shell. Madder or cochineal gives red, indigo with sulphuric acid, blue, onion skins a mottled yellow or brown if the boiling be long continued.

The prepared dyes are however more convenient. Variegated eggs are produced by wrapping them tightly with silk or print and in the boiling process, pattern and color will be transferred to the shell.

If, before boiling, letters, names or dates be written on the shell with grease, that part will not take the color, so white letters will appear on a bright ground.

To write on eggs already colored dip a stick or pencil in strong vinegar or other acid.

Washing the shell with the white of a raw egg gives a good surface for drawing and painting.

The shells may be emptied and then painted or colored and used to hold small gifts.

The shells are first cleaned by washing in vinegar, then the eggs are pierced and a large needle is used to stir up the contents which are then blown out.

After decoration a ribbon is put through the shell or the holes are covered with bright paper.

Tiny cradles for the smallest of dolls can be made by breaking out one quarter of the shell and adding pasteboard rockers.

Half-shells with handles of ribbon or paper make a pretty basket to hold a piece of jewelry.

For a vase glue a large button mold to the shell and paint the whole.

From the custom of giving Easter eggs we have derived the pleasant fashion of sending cards and small gifts at that season. Naturally

---

many of these take the form of the egg, though resembling it in no other way.

The shop windows at this season seem like huge bird-nests filled with all manner of fanciful eggs. These clever imitation eggs have long been an important source of revenue to France and Germany.

There are eggs of all sizes, made of confectionery and more enduring materials, chocolate eggs with cream where the yolk should be, eggs adorned with mottoes, eggs of soap, of glass and china, ostrich eggs for bon-bon boxes, egg-shaped boxes, baskets, and lockets, note paper to imitate egg-shells, etc.

Sofa-pillows and pincushions may take the shape of an egg if they are to serve as presents at Easter-tide.

Another fancy is a penwiper made by gluing two buff worsted balls, one half the size of the other, into an egg-shell.

Give the smaller ball a quill nose and black bead eyes, and the effect will be that of a chicken just leaving his shell.

An egg cosy is a useful addition to the break-fast table.   It is made on the plan of a tea cosy, and is used to keep boiled eggs warm.

A napkin or doily may be embroidered with suitable designs and used for the same purpose.

Engraving on egg shells is another amusement for this season.

With wax stop up the holes in an egg that has been blown.   Write or draw on the outside with tallow or varnish, then cover the whole with vinegar or other weak acid, for a short time.

This removes some of the lime where the shell is not protected by the grease, and the writing becomes very distinct.

In a church in Lisbon, in 1808, during the Spanish war, an egg was found with a prediction against the French on its shell.   The superstitious soldiers thought this was miraculous until the French general had a contradiction of the prophecy engraved on other shells and distributed among them.

A BOTTLED EGG.

Any one unacquainted with the process will be much puzzled to see a whole egg in a bottle, the neck of which has a smaller diameter than the egg.

It is first necessary to soak the egg in vinegar or some acid which will destroy most of the lime of the shell, without injuring its contents. When the shell is softened enough to extend slightly both ways, press it gently in the center and slip into the bottle.

Cover the egg with limewater for a few days to harden the shell again; then pour off the water and leave your friends to wonder how the egg came to be in the bottle.

A DANCING EGG.

Fill a quill with quicksilver and seal at both ends, then thrust it into a hot, hard-boiled egg. As long as the egg is warm, it will dance.

QUEER PEOPLE.

Some very funny people may be made to live in egg shells, for the amusement of children.

Empty the shell by blowing, and pour in melted bees-wax until the egg stands securely on its larger end; a few shot dropped into the warm wax will help matters.

With ink or black paint draw ragged lines near the middle as if the shell were broken there. On the large end sketch the features of an old gentleman and put a tall paper collar just above the ragged line. Draw on the shell or cut from paper and paste in place a pair of arms with hands clasped in front; add feet in the same way. Then put the old fellow on the table and he will stand on his head.

The face may be clouded or serene at the pleasure of the artist, but most people would not feel very happy if standing on their heads.

An old lady can be made in like manner — with the addition of a tissue paper cap.

Another device is a small crying face with jagged lines around it as if the shell were broken a little, but the prisoner could get no further. Or the shell may be filled with wax or clay, and broken away in the place where the face is to be modeled.

Rose buds or tulips can be imitated with good success by painting an egg and gluing on tissue paper or other artificial leaves at the base; an acorn cup will represent the lower part of the calyx.

EGG GAMES.

At the pagan new year festivals many games were played with eggs, and some of them still survive.

Hyde, in his Oriental Sports, says:

" The sport consists in striking their eggs one against another, and the egg that breaks is won by the owner of the one that struck it, and so on."

The Romans had egg-games at their new year, in honor of Castor and Pollux, who were supposed to have come from an egg. These consisted of races in an egg-shaped ring, with eggs for prizes.

An old Saxon chronicle tells of an egg tournament. At suitable distances, in a circle, were placed twelve short poles, and on top of each an egg.

Around this, at full speed, ran the youths armed with blunt lances. The one breaking the most eggs was declared victor. Later, eggs grew too valuable to be wasted, and a similar game was played with wooden rings or balls.

In this country there has of late been a revival of some of these games with other quaint Easter customs.

Many children in days past have matched their eggs or rolled them over the green grass lots in the grounds of the White House at Washington.

Probably the Easter eggs were first boiled hard for greater safety in these games of matching.

At a Paas festival once held in the studio of a New York artist, colored eggs were hung by ribbons from a pussy willow-tree, while quaint little damsels distributed fresh eggs as well as those made of confectionery, from their dainty baskets.

Near Easter time at children's parties the little ones may be sent bird's nesting through the rooms, where the nests are placed in all possible corners, some tucked in bushes or small trees. The nests must be well filled with candy eggs or the real article decorated, and the children must hunt till each finds a nest with his or her own name on it.

THE CASCARONE.

Travelers in Mexico give accounts of an egg game and dance existing there.

The eggs are prepared by first emptying the shells, then refilling them with fine-chopped colored paper, tinsel, mica and sachet powder. The holes are then pasted over with a bit of paper, and the outside is gayly decorated.

In the more prosperous days of Spanish sway, grandees often had the shells filled with gold dust and precious stones. Those times are past, but occasionally small trinkets, coins and candies are mingled.

Several dozen are needed by each participant in the cascarone.

A stranger is at first often startled by having one of these fragile treasure chests broken over his head by a senorita to whom he has not been introduced; but former acquaintance is not considered essential. It is a great compliment to the recipient of the blow, who must return the favor at the first opportunity.

Thrifty matrons intending to give such a ball save all the shells of eggs used in the household and spend their leisure hours in filling and decorating them.

A pretty arrangement of this custom for children's parties was described in WIDE AWAKE for April, 1889.

EGGS IN LITERATURE.

Speculative Philosopher:
　　Whether first the egg, or the hen?
　　Tell me, I pray, ye learned men.
First Scribe:
　　The hen was first, or whence the egg?
　　Give us no more of your doubts, I beg.
Second Scribe:
　　The egg was first, or whence the hen?
　　Tell me how it came or when.

This question which has been deemed worthy of discussion by many writers may have been the Sphinx's riddle.

The origin of our domestic fowls is so ancient that it seems probable that they have always been companions and comforts of mankind. It is certain that they were known and esteemed in India, Persia and Egypt, centuries ago.

Among writers of all ages, the egg has been a favorite illustration.

It is mentioned in several places in the Bible : Deut xxii. 6 ; Job vi. 6 ; Luke xi. 12.

Frequent references to its use as food may be found among the Latin authors.

Plutarch left an elaborate treatise on the question of the precedence of the hen or the egg.

Pliny exalts the medicinal qualities the egg possessed.

Cæsar, Juvenal, Cicero, Martial, Horace and others will be quoted further on respecting the use of eggs as food among the ancient races.

The belief in the mundane egg appears to spread through the traditions of all nations, as do the stories of the deluge.

The Arabian Nights tells of the roc's egg of marvelous size. Similar tales are found in Jewish legends. From one such bird's nest an egg fell which broke, and the white glued three hundred cedar-trees to the ground and over-flowed a village.

Munchausen mentions a kingfisher's nest twice as large as the dome of St. Paul's, which contained five hundred eggs each as large as four hogsheads.

The fables of the woman who killed the hen that laid golden eggs, and of the milkmaid counting her chickens before they were hatched or even she had exchanged her milk for eggs, are full of sound philosophy.

The egg stories among the rhymes of Mother Goose are many. Some like that of Humpty Dumpty are told to children all over the world, in nearly every tongue spoken by man.

It is difficult to trace much real history in the literature of eggs, though one event in America's history is closely connected with an egg story.

The story of Columbus and his critics is too well known to need rehearsal. Any who wish to review it are referred to Washington Irving's Life of Columbus.

There is, however, in the Pacific Ocean an island whose past history may be said to be inclosed in an egg-shell.

This is Easter Island, two thousand miles west of Chili. It is remarkable for its sculptured stones which are said to be the work of the "butterfly king." After the departure of that ruler, elections were decided by contests in egg-gathering. He who first obtained the greatest number being chosen king.

The huts on the island are usually shaped like half-sections of an egg.

It is by no means possible to give here all or even the larger part of the quotations worthy to be gathered on this subject.

Many of these are such terse epigrammatic expressions that they have become proverbs, and their original authors have been lost to sight by their general use.

The egg was a favorite illustration with Shakespeare, and he often uses it to convey some biting sarcasm.

> " An egg or two on holidays at most,
> But their religion ne'er allowed a roast."
>
> Dryden. — *Cock and Fox.*

" The yolke of the egg cannot be without the whyte, nor the whyte without the yolke, no more maye the clergy and the lordes be one without another."   *Berners' Froissart.*

"Lest that ill egg bring forth a cockatrice
To poison all with heresy and vice."
THOS. DUDLEY. 1650.

"So rides he mounted on the market day
Upon a straw-stuffed pannell all the way —
With a maund charged with household mer-
    chandize
With eggs or white meat from both dayries."
BISHOP HALL.

"To helpe it called for a puritan poacht,
That used to turn up the eggs of his eyes."
BEN JONSON.

"Nay, soft and faire, I have eggs on the spit;
I cannot go yet, sir."
Ben JONSON.— *Every Man in His Humour.*
i. e., the eggs need constant turning.

SHAKESPEARE.

"Thy head is as full of quarrels as an egg
is full of meat; and yet thy head hath been
beaten as addle as an egg, for quarrelling."
Romeo and Juliet, Act III. Sc. 1.

"Like egg-shells moved upon their surges,
crack'd as easily against our rocks."
Cymbeline, Act III. Sc. 1.

"Some trick not worth an egg."
Coriolanus, Act IV. Sc. 4.

"And therefore think him as a serpent's egg."
Julius Cæsar, Act II. Sc. 1.

"Even for an egg-shell."
Hamlet, Act IV. Sc. 4.

"Mine honest friend,
Will you take eggs for money?"
Winter's Tale, Act I. Sc. 2.

"I can suck melancholy out of a song, as a
weazel sucks eggs."
As You Like It, Act II. Sc. 5.

"Thou half-penny purse of wit, thou pigeon-
egg of discretion."
Love's Labour's Lost, Act V. Sc. 1.

"Like an ill-roasted egg, all on one side."
As You Like It, Act III. Sc. 2.

"He will steal, sir, an egg out of a cloister."
All's Well That Ends Well, Act IV. Sc. 3.

"If you love an addle egg as well as you love an idle head, you would eat chickens i' the shell."
Troilus and Cressida, Act I. Sc. 2.

"Yet, they say, we are
Almost as like as eggs."
Winter's Tale, Act I. Sc. 2.

Falstaff. "Not so much as will serve to be prologue to an egg and butter."
Henry IV. Part I. Act 1. Sc. 2.

"They are up already, and call for eggs and butter."
Henry IV. Part I. Act II. Sc. 1.

"To her unguarded nest the weasel Scot
Comes sneaking, and so sucks her princely eggs."
Henry V. Act I. Sc. 2.

"Go thou; I'll fetch some flax and whites of eggs to apply to his bleeding face."
Lear, Act III. Sc. 7.

"Thou hadst shiver'd like an egg."
Lear, Act IV. Sc. 6.

Fool. "Give me an egg, nuncle, and I'll give thee two crowns.

Lear. What two crowns shall they be?

Fool. Why, after I have cut the egg i' the middle, and eat up the meat, the two crowns of the egg."
Lear, Act I. Sc. 4.

"What, you egg!
Young fry of treachery!"
Macbeth, Act IV. Sc. 2.

PROVERBS.

THERE'S reason in roasting of eggs.

As full as an egg is of meat.

Don't have too many eggs in one basket.

You cannot teach your grandmother how to suck eggs.

Many people are like eggs; too full of themselves to hold anything else.

We prize more the egg refused us than the ox which is given us.

" Choose eggs of an hour, fish of ten, bread of a day, wine of a year, a woman of fifteen, and a friend of thirty."

" Neither good egg, nor bird."

FROM THE TURKISH.

But yesterday out of the egg; to-day he despises the shell.

Let me cook you an egg,— but the egg is at the vineyard, and the vineyard is on the mountain.

To-day's egg is better than to-morrow's hen.

" An egg and to bed," and, " You must drink as much after an egg as after an ox," show the once popular belief in the indigestibility of eggs.

" I'll warrant you an egg for Easter," is to give assurance of something already certain.

" Better half an egg than the empty shell."

A picture of peace and prosperity is this token from the Beggar's Bush:

" Each man shall eat his own eggs and butter In his own shade and sunshine."

The small value of eggs is variously expressed :

" Who will take eggs for money ? " or, " You will get eggs for your money," or " He gave me eggs for money."

" O, rogue, rogue! I shall have eggs for my money ; I must lay myself."

" As dear as two eggs a penny," indicates a bad bargain, as also, " You come with your five eggs a penny and four of them be rotten."

"To come with five eggs," signified to make a foolish remark, in the time of Sir Thomas More's Utopia: "Whiles another gyveth counsell to make pease with the Kynge of Arragone, another commeth in wyth hyse v eggs."

He that buys eggs, buys many shells. "Give him the other half-egg, and burst him."

"Purposes, like eggs, unless they be hatched into action, will run into decay."

SMILES.

"Enjoy spare feast! a radish and an egg."

COWPER.

"It's very hard to shave an egg."

GEO. HERBERT. — *Jacula Prudentum.*

"Now's the only bird lays eggs of gold."

J. R. LOWELL. — *Hosea Bigelow.*

"Things said for conversation are chalk eggs."

R. W. EMERSON.

"Tom, my boy, this world is hollow as an egg-shell."

H. B. STOWE.

"The greatest event in a hen's life is made up of an egg and a cackle."

H. W. BEECHER.

"And eggs — even they have their moral. See how they come and go. Every pleasure is transitory. We can't even eat long."

DICKENS, *in Martin Chuzzlewit.*

"A mystery hatched out of an egg and just as mysterious as if the egg had been addle."

HAWTHORNE.

"All this noise on account of an egg. The children have picked up an egg? Great good will it do them. There is not very much in an egg. God provides them for everybody."

TOLSTOI.

"No more egg-pop made with eggs that would have been fighting cocks to judge by the pugnacity the beverage containing their yolks developed."

O. W. HOLMES. — *Essays.*

"I try his head occasionally as housewives try eggs — give it an intellectual shake and hold it up to the light, so to speak, to see if it has life in it actual or potential or only contains lifeless albumen."

Autocrat of the Breakfast Table.

"I think that a hen who undertakes to lay 2 eggs a day must necessarily neglect sum other branch of bizzness."

JOSH BILLINGS.

"Ay, touch it with a tender touch,
    For, till the egg is biled,
Who knows but that unwittingly
    It may be smashed and spiled?
The summer breeze that 'gainst it blows
    Ought to be stilled and hushed,
For eggs like youthful purity,
    Are 'orful' when they're squushed."
    From a Tender Lay on a New-laid Egg.

ROMANCES OF EGGS.

N the good old times Easter eggs were often adorned with tiny pictures or emblematical devices and sentimental mottoes. Such eggs did duty as valentines, and were afterward preserved in the homes of the happy pairs. That the inscription might be read without touching the frail treasure, the egg was often kept in a glass. The dates on these eggs were considered as reliable evidence as those from a tombstone.

The new fashion of egg photographs is but a revival of this old custom.

Many lovers of the present day have been made happy by receiving an Easter egg bearing a photograph of their sweethearts.

Photographs of distinguished persons are often pasted on Easter eggs and sent to their friends or more often their enemies. A patriotic German would hardly care to receive a

Boulanger egg, or a Frenchman one bearing Bismarck's face.

An iron egg is to be seen in one of the grandest of the European museums, which was once sent as a betrothal gift from a prince to a princess.

The lady angry at so mean a present, flung it to the floor, when a spring opened showing a silver lining, a second opening revealed a yolk of gold, and a third and fourth displayed diamonds and rubies, by which the lady's displeasure was soon assuaged.

"The marriage *aux œufs*," between Marguerite of Austria, gouvernante of Flanders, and Philibert the Handsome, Duke of Savoy, is a still more romantic story.

It was the custom on Easter Monday in the district of Bresse to scatter a hundred eggs on a level place, covered by sand. Then a lad and lass, hand in hand, would execute the dance of the country. If they succeeded without breaking an egg they were considered affianced, even if it were against their parents' will.

On this occasion three couples had tried in

vain, but Savoy and Austria accomplished the dance without crushing a single shell. When Philibert said, "Let us adopt the custom of Bresse," Marguerite suffered her hand to remain in his, and history tells us that their married life was long and happy.

COMMERCIAL STATISTICS.

HE egg trade differs from most other branches of business; the supply is limited, while the demand is almost unlimited.

Small flocks of poultry are almost always more profitable than large ones. This affords a better opportunity for undertaking the egg business, as a large capital is not required.

The census returns do not give a full report of the egg production of the United States, but furnish the figures of those which are bought and sold; perhaps an equal quantity is consumed by the producers.

In 1879, according to the tenth census, the number of eggs produced was 456,910,916 dozen. At fifteen cents per dozen, the egg crop would amount to $68,536,637.

The consumption of one egg daily by each inhabitant of the United States could hardly be thought an extravagant estimate.   This would amount to over four million dozen.

That there may be no reason for disputing his figures, Edward Atkinson puts one half an egg as the daily average, and counts the cost as only one cent each; even then the value of the annual egg crop would be about one hundred million dollars.   This sum is more than the value of the annual product of silver or pig-iron or wool.

The poultry and egg crop together are estimated to be worth two hundred and fifty million dollars annually to the United States.   And yet we import annually forty-eight million dozen eggs from Canada, France, Germany, Austria and Denmark.

During the last four months of 1888, 6708 cases, each containing fifty dozen, were thus brought into the United States.   This will continue until poultry raisers demand a duty on foreign eggs.

Warner Miller (*N. Y. Weekly Tribune*, Mar. 28, 1888) says: "Farmers' letters are almost unanimous in urging increase of duties on eggs, having the impression that eggs are now dutiable. They are not — they are admitted free. Though imports are small, they have affected prices on the sea board and Canada border. Farmers' wives and children would be glad of the two million dollars yearly sent abroad for eggs.

"Eggs come from France and Belgium (China 107,275 dozen, in 1887), England, Germany, Mexico and specially Canada whence (1887) 13,682,000 dozen. Exports never have reached four hundred thousand dozen.

IMPORTS AND EXPORTS FROM 1877 TO 1887

DATE	IMPORTS DOZ.	EXP. DOZ.	DATE	IMPORTS DOZ.	EXP. DOZ.
1877	5,048,271	32,591	1883	15,277,065	300,023
1878	6,053,649	94,265	1884	16,488,507	295,484
1879	6,022,506	91,740	1885	16,099,410	240,768
1880	7,773,492	85,885	1886	15,992,642	212,202
1881	9,578,071	80,146	1887	13,930,054	372,912
1882	11,928,784	146,776			

"A duty of five cents per dozen will inconvenience only foreigners."

Imported eggs are sold in all large cities in the East and North, mainly to packers and manufacturers.

New York City takes about one fifteenth of the entire crop. For the year ending October 31, 1887, New York received 59,095,330 dozen, and imported also fifty thousand dozen.

In January, 1889, 57,653 barrels, each containing sixty-five to seventy dozen eggs, were received in New York, against 37,103 barrels during the same month in 1888. The increase was largely due to the mild winter.

Chicago, in 1888, received 624,721 cases, each case containing thirty dozen, and shipped 460,060 cases.

Philadelphia, in 1887, had 501,245 cases, or 15,037,350 dozen.

The San Francisco report is incomplete, but shows about four million dozen.

Figures from the Boston Chamber of Commerce give the annual receipts of eggs in that city as follows:

1885	. .	10,000,000 dozen.
1886	. .	12,000,000 "
1887	. .	13,500,000 "
1888	. .	14,100,000 "

A part of these find a market outside the city, but are balanced by the quantity brought in by small dealers.

Carroll D. Wright, in the Massachusetts Census of 1885, gives figures which show the rapid increase in the demand and supply of eggs.

In 1855, poultry and eggs, $52,688.

In 1885, eggs alone, $1,615,582.

Of the total number — 7,072,187 1-2 dozen — Bristol and Worcester counties produce 1,000,000 dozen each, and Middlesex ranks next.

Great Britain receives eggs from France, Germany, Spain, Portugal and the Azores; eggs valued at from $10,000,000 to $15,000,000 ($1,000,000 per month).

In 1875 the value of the eggs imported was £2,559,860.

French eggs are often retailed in England within a week after they are laid.

In 1813 France sent to England 1,754,140 eggs. In 1878 there came from the Continent 391,174,000,000 eggs.

Berlin requires about 200,000,000 eggs yearly.

The estimate of food per capita in Paris, as annually published, allows each person fifteen dozen or 180 eggs.

Soyer estimated that the average man consumed 24,000 eggs in his lifetime.

Large bakeries or biscuit factories use often 80,000 eggs daily.

An ocean steamer takes 15,000 to 20,000 for each trip.

Hotels use from 1000 to 5000 eggs every day.

Gladstone, as reported by the London Live Stock Journal (five years ago), says:

"I will now take another case — that of eggs; that is a very good illustration, for it is in everybody's power to rear poultry, and, if I may say, grow eggs.

In 1855, though that was a time when freedom of trade had advanced largely in the country, and when there was, consequently, a very great increase in the consumption of good food by the people, 100,000,000 eggs were imported from abroad, which represented a consumption of an average of $3\frac{1}{2}$ foreign eggs to every man, woman and child.

You might have said, if asked to send eggs: 'O, no! there are already plenty or more than enough in the market.'

But that is not the fact, for in 1880 the import had increased to 750,000,000 eggs from foreign countries.

It is hardly credible, so vast and so multiplied is the demand for these little but very useful commodities, every one of them helping to feed somebody.

The consumption per head has increased from $3\frac{1}{2}$ to no fewer than $26\frac{1}{2}$ eggs.

That illustrates what I have said to you about the enormous, insatiable capacity of the human stomach. Depend upon it, that if it be in your power to turn your attention — I do not say at first on a very large but on a moderate scale — to the production of those articles which are of the nature of comforts, or even comparative luxuries, for popular consumption, you will see that gradually the market will open and adjust itself for their reception.

I think the figures I have quoted are a distinct proof of the truth and reality of what I have said."

Statistics also show that the Northern States, particularly New England, produce the largest number of eggs from a given number of hens.

This is probably due to the greater care and variety of food given the hens, since the milder climate of the South ought to favor the production of eggs.

Most of the eggs used in large hotels in Florida, and elsewhere in the South, are sent from the Northern States.

Large eggs naturally bring the highest price, and will continue to do so as long as eggs are sold by count instead of weight.

In some places it is now customary to sell eggs by the pound, and when this practice prevails cookery will become a more exact science.

Eggs are often sorted or sized, like fruit, by passing through a ring.

The average weight is as follows :

Hens eggs	$1\frac{1}{2}$	to 2 ounces.
Ducks "	2	to 3 "
Turkey "	3	to 4 "
Goose "	4	to 6 "

WEIGHT AND PRODUCTION OF EGGS.

P. L. Simmonds, before the London Society of Arts:

"The standard yield and weight of eggs for the different varieties of the domestic fowl may be taken as follows: Light Brahmas and Partridge Cochins, eggs seven to the pound; they lay, according to treatment and food, from eighty to one hundred and fifty per annum; sometimes more if kept well. Dark Brahmas, eight to the pound, seventy per annum."

	TO THE POUND	PER ANNUM
Black, White and Buff Cochins	8	100
Plymouth Rocks	8	100
Houdan *	8	150
La Fleche	7	130
Black Spanish	7	150
Dominiques	9	130
Game Fowl	9	130
Creves	7	130
Leghorns	9	150 to 200
Hamburgs	9	170
Polish	9	150
Bantams	16	60
Turkeys	6	35 to 60
Ducks	5 to 6	
Geese	4	20
Guinea Fowl	11	60

* Non-sitters

NATIONAL BUTTER, CHEESE AND EGG ASSOCIATION.

The report of the Committee on Packing and Preserving Eggs:

"It is very evident that the salvation, prosperity and future confidence in this trade depends on substituting the weight of twenty-four ounces for ten eggs as a standard of quality or value, instead of counting as at present.　.　.

"This is not all of it; for the more healthy Northern egg will greatly outsell the lighter, weaker and more sickly Southern egg.　The old, dried-up, withered remnant of an egg, now so common, will not linger to plague the consumer and commission man.

"Eggs laid by birds and small guinea-hens will, when sold by actual weight, become a curiosity in the market instead of being as now often sold as a subterfuge for food."

TESTS OF THE FRESHNESS OF EGGS.

THE perishable nature of eggs is their greatest disadvantage.

Though many experiments have been tried, as yet no practical method has been discovered for keeping eggs in their original freshness for any great length of time.

An "egg tester" is a little instrument for holding an egg directly before a strong light, which is obtained by an arrangement of mirrors; this is convenient, but not essential.

Fresh eggs are transparent throughout; old ones only at the top, and dark spots appear in the center. If held before a bright light these spots appear; therefore this process is called "candling" by egg-dealers.

The specific gravity of the fresh egg is greater than that of water. (Hence is used as a test of solutions.)

As the egg grows older it loses water by

evaporation through the pores of the shell and takes in more air. Hence the smaller the air cell the fresher the egg. Fresh eggs will sink in pure water, and if salt be added to the water the proof of their purity will be still stronger. Uncertain ones will stand on one end, while bad ones will float.

If totally bad, a large portion of the contents of an egg are in a gaseous state, and therefore it is very light, while a fresh egg is heavy; eggs may thus be compared in the hand.

When an egg rattles if shaken, it is of doubtful freshness; for this shows that the air space is large and the inner lining loose.

This is not a desirable test, since such treatment might break the yolk bag or the skin lying next the shell, and in either case hasten the decomposition.

Another test is to place the large end against the tongue. If slightly warm it indicates that the shell is full and the contents good; if cold, that that end of the shell is empty, and life extinct.

When any number of eggs is to be used in

cooking it is best to break them separately, to avoid spoiling all by one bad one.

The shell of a fresh egg is often rougher than that of a stale one; but the eggs of different breeds differ in this respect.

PRESERVATION OF EGGS.

IR and heat are the two chief agents in the decomposition of eggs, as of all animal substances.

Almost anything that will exclude the air from the egg will aid in its preservation, provided it be kept in a cool place and in an upright position, so that the yolk shall not adhere to the shell.

It is not usually desirable to preserve eggs for the markets, since the fresh article always brings better prices; but frugal housekeepers when eggs are low in price may provide a supply for winter use when market prices double.

Limed eggs may be found in the markets at several cents per dozen less than fresh, and other preserved eggs come under the same class.

The lime, however, is apt to eat the shell; to give a slight taste to the whole egg, and often hardens the yolk and turns it red.

A reliable formula for the lime water is this :

One pint of salt and one pint of lime dissolved in three or four gallons of hot water; two ounces of cream of tartar is sometimes added. Boil all together and skim, and when cold cover the eggs with it. A stone jar is the best thing to pack them in.

The lime fills the pores in the egg-shell, and thus keeps it air-tight.

Borax water made in the proportion of one heaping teaspoonful of borax to one pint of boiling water also makes the shell air-tight.

A solution of silicate of soda acts chemically with the lime of the shell, excluding the air.

An easier, but effectual method is to coat the egg with any kind of fat or oil ; olive, cotton or linseed oils, or lard or beef or mutton fat. It was the old custom along the Mississippi River to pack eggs in barrels of lard; when they had reached their destination eggs and lard were separated and both sold. In Russia the eggs are packed small end down, and melted tallow poured over them.

The grease fills the air-holes and keeps out the air, but its tendency to grow rancid is a disadvantage.

A mixture of one third bees-wax and two thirds oil, olive or cotton-seed, warmed together, is also recommended.

Vaseline has been used, melted with three per cent. salicylic acid.

The Chinese method of preserving eggs is to dip in melted wax.

Varnish or gum arabic may be used in the same fashion.

The white of egg rubbed over the outside fills the shell to the exclusion of the air.

At a poultry show held not long ago in England, the first prize for preserved eggs was awarded to those which had been packed in salt. Yet sometimes the eggs absorb too much salt.

Sawdust, ashes, baked earth, sand and powdered charcoal have all been used successfully for packing eggs.

In England, at a dairy show held in 1884, the first premium for preserved eggs was given to those which had been dipped in gum arabic; the second, to eggs rubbed in lard and packed in salt.

A comparison of eggs treated with lime-water, others with a paste of chalk and water, and others with diluted white of egg and water-glass, showed the latter to be the best method of preserving the original flavor.

Eggs dipped in linseed oil have in six months lost only three per cent. of their original weight, while those not treated at all had lost eighteen per cent.

Dr. Hunter, in his *Culina*, has said: "Boil one minute to keep a year."

This is the easiest way of all for the average housekeeper.

Put fresh eggs in a wire basket and hold in boiling water while counting six, being sure that the water touches every part alike. This hardens the white of the egg lying close to the shell, and that keeps out the air. Let them cool, wipe dry and pack in oats, ashes or salt, and they may be kept a year.

The eggs may each be closely wrapped in paper after treatment, or the paper alone is a great protection, as it is nearly air-tight.

Dealers sometimes use boards, with holes small enough to prevent the eggs slipping through, but large enough to keep them upright.

More often egg-cases are supplied with paste-board divisions, each space large enough to hold an egg.

AUSTRALIAN METHOD OF PRESERVING EGGS.

Glass jars with patent stoppers having vulcanized India rubber joints, making them perfectly air-tight, are used.

These jars are placed in hot water until the air in them is warm and rarefied.

As soon as the eggs are collected they are wrapped in paper to prevent knocking, and are placed in the warm jars, with the pointed ends up. The jars are immediately closed up, and then removed from the hot water.

If this process is skillfully carried out the eggs will be fit for the table months afterward. The secret is to heat the air in the jars thoroughly; the papers may be baked and used warm.

Any stopper will do that excludes the air.

Dessicated or portable eggs have been prepared for market to some extent.

Beaten egg is evaporated at a temperature of one hundred and twenty-five degrees Fahrenheit, till perfectly dry and hard. It is then packed, and when wanted for use, three parts of cold water are added to one part egg. Blood albumen and chromate of lead are often used to adulterate eggs thus prepared.

Messrs. Effner & Co., of Passau, Bavaria, prepare this egg-meat, of the best quality, by using only the best eggs.

It is said to be perfectly satisfactory for cakes and omelets.

Though a great convenience for travelers, it will hardly take the place of fresh eggs.

This preparation somewhat resembles gelatine in appearance, consisting of crystallized particles, of but ten per cent. or fifteen per cent. of the original weight.

The main points to remember in preserving eggs, are:

1.   That heat hastens either decay or development.

2.   That anything that excludes the air, provided it will not affect the flavor of the egg, may be used in packing.

3.   That however carefully preserved, it must not be expected that they be equal in flavor to fresh eggs.

Eggs may be kept in a cool, dark place where they cannot freeze, for three months, without other protection than being placed in an upright position.   They should be reversed occasionally, to prevent the yolk from adhering to the shell.

USE OF EGGS IN ARTS AND MANUFACTURES.

THE shell of emu and ostrich eggs are often used as drinking cups and cooking utensils by the natives; and necklaces are made of pieces of shell. They are also decorated and mounted as vases.

Powdered shells are used in the manufacture of imitation ivory.

The adhesive nature of the white makes it a useful glue or cement, especially when mixed with brick dust, plaster of Paris, gum mastic, lime, or the Chinese use it with powdered glass to mend China.

The albumen of the egg white is largely used as a varnish for cards and paintings, and in photography and calico printing.

The Alsatians alone use thirty-eight million annually.

The white of egg is also used in making court plaster; the luster of morocco leather is restored by it; gold leaf is applied to leather by its aid, and grease is removed from leather by one or two applications.

The yolk is used to render oils diffusible in water; from it Russia, a valuable oil, is extracted, which is used in manufacture of the Kazan soap. Before the discovery of oil colors, the yolk was used by painters, as in the Chapter House at Westminster.

In the preparation of the finest leather the yolks are used, the oil giving to kid the softness so esteemed in gloves, one egg being used for each skin.

That the value of eggs for clarifying various substances has long been known is shown by one entry, in the year 1350, in the household books of the French court, of eggs to clarify sugar. At the present time in France, wine clarifiers use eighty million annually.

There is a legitimate use for bad eggs, though the natural association of ideas connect them only with riots. Some firms make a business of collecting ancient eggs from large dealers. After opening they are classified by age. The yolks of the better grades are used by morocco dressers, the whites in some kinds of confectionery, while the very bad are used in tanneries for polishing leather.

THE CHEMISTRY OF THE EGG.

STANDARD authorities give the following proportions of chemical elements in the dry substance of the average hen's egg; other eggs show but slight variations :

Carbon . .	53 to 55	per cent.
Nitrogen . .	15 to 16	" "
Hydrogen .	7	" "
Oxygen . .	21 to 22	" "
Sulphur . .	1 to 2	" "
Phosphorus .	5	" "

A more practical form of analysis is this :

EGGS		BEEF	
Water . .	74	Water . .	64
Proteid . .	12.5	Proteid . .	14
Fat . . .	12	Fat . . .	21
Salts . . .	1	Salts . . .	1

Dr. Pavy quotes from Letheby these figures:

	WATER	ALBUMEN	FATS	SALTS
Entire egg	74	14	10.5	1.5
Yolk	52	16	30.7	1.3
White	78	20.4		1.6

König gives for the different parts of the egg:

	WATER	NUT. SUB.	FAT	ASH
Whole egg	74	12.5	12	1
White of egg	85.5	13	0.25	0.5
Yolk " "	51	16	31.5	1

The average egg weighs a trifle less than two ounces. Seven to ten are required for one pound.

1 lb. shelled eggs:

	OZ.	GR.
Water	12	66
Proteid	2	0
Fat	1	240
Salts		418

Reckoning the weight at two ounces, and deducting one tenth for the weight of the shell, the dry constituents of the egg would be :

Nitrogenous matter	110 gr.
Fatty "	82 "
Saline "	11 "

A trace of sugar is often present in the egg, also of soda and starch.

The type of all nitrogenous foods is albumen, found in its purest natural form in the white of the egg. It corresponds to the fibrine of meat, the gluten of grains and the caseine of milk.

The presence of sulphur is shown by the black stain which appears on silver spoons used with eggs. While fresh it may be removed by salt; afterward by rubbing with whiting.

The offensive smell of aged eggs is caused by the combination of the hydrogen in the air with the sulphur and phosphorus of the egg.

By observation and experiments scientists have found that certain fungi will develop in eggs, since the unbroken shells may be penetrated by liquids which introduce the germs.

If the shells are dry these fungi cannot flourish, but if moist, they send long fibers through the pores of the shell.

Sometimes they give the egg a similar appearance to that caused by the boiling process.

The temperature of one hundred and four degrees Fahrenheit, sustained for three weeks time, is sufficient to hatch eggs. Their vitality has been retained after exposure to ten degrees Fahrenheit.

"It is a remarkable fact that the freezing point of new-laid eggs is much lower than that of the water and albumen of which they principally consist, both of which congeal at about the same temperature."

Appleton's American Cyclopædia.

Egg albumen coagulates when exposed to heat, alcohol, strong acids or metallic salts.

Experiments with white of egg have shown that it begins to cook at one hundred and thirty-four degrees Fahrenheit, while at one hundred and sixty degrees it becomes a solid mass; at two hundred and twelve degrees it shrinks and begins to grow horny. A greater degree of heat will render albumen too hard to be easily digested. Hence eggs will cook after they are taken from the fire until cooled to one hundred and thirty or one hundred and forty degrees Fahrenheit.

THE FOLLOWING POINTS ARE TO BE REMEMBERED IN ALL COOKING OF EGGS.

The fresher the eggs the more time required for cooking, since they then contain a greater proportion of water, and since albumen requires higher temperature in proportion as it is diluted with water.

Albumen, the main substance of the egg, requires less cooking and a lower degree of heat than starch, therefore they should not usually be combined unless the latter has been previously cooked.

Eggs cook at such a low temperature that they are used to protect other articles.
A coating of beaten egg quickly becomes hard and helps the food thus covered to keep its shape and retain its juices.

To clarify liquids like syrups, jellies, soups and coffee, egg albumen has no equal.
Mix with the cold liquid the white and shells of eggs, one or two to each quart, and stir the mixture until it is ready to boil. After five minutes uninterrupted boiling cool and strain.

The adhesive nature of the albumen causes it to stick to all tiny particles which float, making the liquid turbid ; heat then coagulates it, making it settle to the bottom, carrying the particles with it and leaving the liquid clear. Some light substances will rise on top in the form of scum.

For coffee, mix egg-shells, ground coffee and a little cold water before adding boiling water.

If too much egg be used the full strength of the coffee will not be obtained, the albumen preventing its escape. Egg-shells, therefore, wiped clean before breaking, are sufficient to make the coffee clear if one or two are used for one quart.

MEDICINE.

HE commonness of the egg makes it a valuable remedy when others could not be obtained. If swallowed at once a raw egg will detach a fish-bone which has lodged in the throat.

Whites of eggs taken immediately after certain poisons will render them harmless; such as salts of lead, mercury, copper and acid poisons. The white of one egg will neutralize four grains of corrosive sublimate. It should be mixed with water and drank.

The albumen is coagulated by the poison and wraps it in an insoluble covering, thus protecting the delicate coatings of the stomach until the patient is relieved by vomiting.

A French method of administering castor oil (cod liver, likewise) is to first warm it, stir in an egg, cook slightly, flavor with salt, sugar or acid jelly. The bitter taste of quinine may be disguised by mixing it with the white of an egg.

An oil is made from the yolk, which in Russia is considered almost miraculous in its healing properties.

The eggs are boiled hard, the yolks crushed, heated and stirred till the whole mass is almost ready to take fire, when each yolk will yield two or more teaspoonfuls of the oil.

Or, one part raw yolk is beaten with two parts water, one part alcohol is then added and the mixture left until the oil floats.

Or, the dry yolk is crushed, and digested in alcohol or ether, becomes colorless, while a bright yellow oil, about two thirds the whole weight of the dry yolk, is extracted.

The bites of insects are made easier by a plaster of the yolk of an egg and salt.

The yolk and spirits of turpentine are used as a salve.

The whole of a raw egg, or the yolk alone, may be rubbed into the hair occasionally to stimulate its growth and prevent falling off; wash thoroughly with soft water afterwards.

For tan or sunburn, the juice of one lemon and white of one egg may be slightly cooked together and applied at night; the mixture is soft and cooling.

Egg and lemon juice beaten together are recommended for hoarseness. It has long been thought that eggs were good for the voice. Charles II. of England presented a favorite singer with a silver egg filled with guineas, saying: "Take this; I am told that eggs are good for the voice."

Beat the whites of two eggs with two table-spoonfuls of cream, sweeten, and add one half teaspoonful of powdered gum arabic; swallow slowly for sore throat.

Mixed with honeyed wine and oil of roses, yolk of egg was an early remedy for diseased eyes. The white of egg and plantain water is sometimes used for inflamed eyes.

Alum curd, made by mixing white of egg with alum, is used in medicine as an astringent poultice.

Mustard for plasters, if mixed with white of egg, will do its work without blistering.

The white of egg is an excellent application to exclude the air from any place where the skin is broken, especially for burns and scalds. Several coatings are necessary to exclude the air. It is more cooling than sweet oil.

The skin of an egg is sometimes used for boils, or wherever the skin is grazed it forms a finer plaster than any that can be applied.

Allopath and homeopath both find that egg-shells calcined at low heat give the purest form of carbonate of lime. The animal composition being better suited to the human stomach than chalk. It is used as an antiacid, and is a valuble absorbent.

The powdered shells are used as tooth powder.

Raw and hard-boiled eggs are the best of foods for young fishes, birds and sick animals.

EGGS AS FOOD.

THE use of eggs for food may be said to be a direct interference with the intentions of nature, yet it may likewise be taken as an indication of the advance of civilization.

> " Look at the polished nations hight,
> The civilized, the most polite,
> Is that which bears the praise of nations
> For dressing eggs two hundred fashions,
> Whereas at savage feeders look —
> The less refined — the less they cook."
>
> HOOD.

The custom of ancient shepherds in the far East was to place the raw egg in a sling, which was then whirled round and round until the heat produced by the rapid motion had cooked the egg within.

From this primitive method to the elaborate concoctions of modern cooks (who even use the perfumes of flowers as flavors for omelets and the like), there is a great advance. For these variations, we are indebted to the experiments of French cooks, who by changes of sauces and seasoning could serve eggs in a different fashion every day in the year.

"Though many, I own, are the evils they've
      brought us,
Though royalty's there on her very last legs,
Yet who can help loving the land that has
      taught us,
Six hundred and eighty-five ways to dress eggs?
MOORE.

The Romans began their cœna, or supper, the distinctively family meal, with eggs as a relish, and closed with fruit. Horace therefore uses the phrase, "*Ab ovo usque ad mala*" (from the egg to the apples), to signify from the beginning to the end of the feast.

Juvenal speaks of —

" The largest Eggs yet warm within their nest,
Together with the Hens which laid them drest."

Utensils found in Pompeii make it plain that eggs were favorites there ; in a painting from the walls of one of the excavated houses, a row of egg-yolks appear as a decoration of some dish upon the dining-table.

According to Cæsar, the flesh of fowls was a forbidden food in Briton ; though it was freely used by the conquerors. The Saxons, however, kept many geese and ate their eggs, but thought it sacrilege to eat the flesh of a bird which furnishes such desirable food while living.

In the thirteenth century, from a history of the street cries of Paris, we learn that eggs were hawked in that city.

They appear to have been used as food in all ages, though the price of three pence for two dozen, which was fixed by the English Parliament of the fourteenth century, shows either that they were not in great demand, or were very abundant.

Among the dishes of the fifteenth century, in which eggs figured largely, were the jussell made of eggs and grated bread, and seasoned with saffron and sage. The froise was a sort of omelet, in which strips of bacon appeared. The tansy was another omelet, seasoned with chopped herbs.

Eggs were also used in caudles — a sort of custard — and in the wassail.

The cooks of that age had a fancy for glazing their dishes with raw egg-yolk, which process was known as endowing.

Eggs with green sauce were served at Gray's Inn on Easter Day.

Eggs and bacon were commonly combined in Chaucer's time.

Buttered eggs, the ancestor of scrambled eggs and similar entrées, was a common dish in England in early times, according to the household books of the noblemen.

Shakespeare mentions this mixture as a common food with country carriers.

Massinger, in the *City Madam*, says :
" Men may talk of country Christmasses,
Their thirty-pound buttered eggs and their pies
          of carp's tongues."

Sir Kenelm Digby speaks of buttering eggs
with cream. He also tells of a Chinese drink
where eggs are used.

" The Jesuit that came from China, A. D.
1664, told Mr. Waller that to a drachm of tea
they put a pint of water, and frequently take
the yolks of two new-laid eggs and beat them
up with as much fine sugar as is sufficient for the
tea, and stir all well together."

A phrase occurring in many recipes in the Har-
leian MSS. is : " Take faire zolks of eyren and the
white, and drawe them through a streynour."

In the Douce MS. directions are given for
making the sops mentioned by early authors.

" Take mylke and boyle it, and thanne tak
yolkys of eyroun (eggs), ytryid (separated) fro
the whyte, and hete it, but let it nowt boyle,
and stere it well tyl it be somwhat thikke ;
thanne caste therto salt and sugre, and kytte

fayre paynemaynnys in round soppys, and caste the soppys theron, and serve it forth for a potage."

The *Forme of Cury* is the title of a collection of recipes made by the master cooks of Richard II. about 1390. Among these is the following:

TREDURE.

Take brede and grate it. Make a lyre (mixture) of raw ayrenn (eggs) and do thereto, safron and powder douce (allspice) and lye it up with gode broth, and make it as a cawdel and do thereto a lytel verjous.

In another recipe this phrase is found:

And if it be not in Lent, alye (mix) it with zolkes of eyren (eggs).

The remaining recipes are taken from a MS. compiled early in the fourteenth century.

CREM BOYLED.

Take crem of cowe mylke, and zolkes of egges, and bete hom wel togedur, and do hit in a pot, and let hit boyle tyl hit be stondynge, and do therto sugur, and colour hit with saffron, and dresse hit forthe in leches, and plante therin flowres of borage, or of vyolet.

BRUET OF EGGES.

Take faire watur, and let hit boyle, then do therin butter and gobettes of chese, and let it sethe togedur; take egges and wringe hom thurgh a streynour, and bete hom wel togedur and medel hit wel with verjous, and do hit in the pot, but let hit not boyle, and do thereto pouder and serve hit forthe.

1326–1399. Early MS.

Eggs were once thought to be hard to digest; possibly this was the result of the articles with which they were combined.

Dr. Arbuthnot, Pope's friend, said:
"Eggs are perhaps the highest and most nourishing of all animal food, and the most indigestible."

Experiments of later date prove that an egg is usually digested sooner than a potato and quite as soon as beef or mutton.

Hard-boiled eggs require 3 hours 30 minutes
Soft   "   "   "   3   "
Fried   .   "   "   3   "   30   "
Roasted   "   "   2   "   15   "
Raw   "   "   2   "
Raw (beaten) "   "   1   "   30   "

That life can be sustained by so little nourishment as a single egg daily is proved by the experience of a German scholar who took refuge from a hostile enemy in a loft. A hen laid her daily egg for two weeks, and this was all his food, yet when the army had gone he had strength to reach home.

A similar story is told of a refugee from the massacre of St. Bartholomew.

Eggs are claimed to be promoters of longevity. Of the Duke of Newcastle, in the reign of

Charles I., it is said: " His supper consists of an egg and a draft of small beer. By this temperance he finds himself very healthful, and may yet live many years, being now seventy-three."

Ericsson the inventor, whose work, continued to old age, was of the kind usually exhaustive of vital force, practised rigid abstemiousness.

Laboring, at least twelve hours out of the twenty-four, his breakfast for each day of the year was two poached eggs. He adhered to this till almost the end of his busy life.

Other men laboring with body and brain have found eggs very sustaining food. Weston, the pedestrian, while walking one hundred miles in twenty-two hours, consumed from sixteen to twenty raw eggs.

Estimates based on experiments claim that with pork at ten cents per pound, and eggs at twenty-four cents per dozen, one bushel of corn will produce three dollars worth of eggs, and only one third as much pork. Add to this fact the disagreeable work necessary in the care of the pig and his conversion into pork, the scale hangs heavy in favor of poultry rather than pig.

If for every pig kept by private families, a flock of hens was substituted, there would be less patent medicine required, and a general improvement in the health.

Without denying the merits of the pig, especially his contribution to the bean-pot, may it not be true that if he who drinks beer, thinks beer, he who eats pig often acts pig?

The Jews, who taboo pork, are a remarkably healthy race. As a people they make great use of eggs, even the poorest giving them preference over other food.

Many vegetarians allow themselves milk and eggs, and as a class are wonderfully free from illness.

One of our best known poets, a country-bred man (Whittier) has said (*Harper's Monthly*, February, 188–):

"I think that is the reason why the present generation is not so strong as the former. It is owing to the way the parents lived, eating so much pork and potatoes."

A missionary to one of the islands of the Pacific, when urged to partake of native dainties, rather than refuse all such hospitality, always ventured to eat a boiled egg, since that could not fail to be clean inside. Other travelers have sought the same refuge.

Some savage tribes think eggs unfit for food, and never dreamed of eating them until they saw the missionaries do so. In the Pacific, many islanders save eggs to sell to the ships, but never use them themselves.

Mr. Drummond, in his *Tropical Africa*, says: "Eggs are never eaten by the natives, but are always set."

Dr. M. L. Holbrook writes: "I have only just received a letter from a Hindoo who states that he does not remember to have ever eaten an egg."

Pundita Ramabai, having been reared in a faith which does not allow the taking of life to supply food — or the destruction of the germ of the egg — though she has accepted Christian teachings, cannot yet bring herself to eat meats or foods containing eggs.

It has been said that " there is no egg of bird known, which is not good for food, or which could not be eaten by a hungry man."

Fewer individuals have been known to have an antipathy for eggs than for most foods ; no honest appetite rejects them.

Liebig asserted that the eggs of birds furnish the most complete nutriment, since they contain in fair proportion, all the elements needed to sustain life.

KINDS AND QUALITIES OF EGGS.

THOUGH they differ in flavor with the kind of bird and its food, their composition is similar.

Like milk, eggs suffer in quality if the food of the animal is inferior.

Pale yolks are generally caused by lack of proper food. Hens fed on corn produce bright yellow yolks.

If hens are fed on fish the eggs will be strong-flavored and poor.

" Choose eggs oblong, remember they'll be
    found,
Of sweeter taste and whiter than the round."

HORACE.

The recipes given further on apply mainly to hens' eggs, but others may be substituted with due regard to differences in size or weight and flavor.

Ducks' eggs are rather richer and usually cook quicker than those of turkey and geese.

The plover's eggs are considered a delicacy, and are consequently high priced. Swans' eggs are occasionally used.

A single ostrich egg is quite a feast, since its contents equal those of twenty-eight hens' eggs. It requires an hour's cooking, and then is said to be very good eating.
The shell, which holds three pints, is often bored and used for decorative purposes.

Albatross eggs are eaten by the aborigines in New Zealand.

The gathering of eggs of sea-birds is a regular business, having curious laws and customs, and requires much courage, as it is full of danger. These eggs are usually strong, and contain much oil, and are only suited to vigorous stomachs. The eggs of the guillemot, stork and cormorant are often eaten.

The larger the egg the larger the bird is a

general truth; the apteryx of New Zealand is, however, an exception. Birds which quit the nest soon after hatching are more fully developed when hatched, hence come from a larger egg.

That birds have existed whose eggs were of enormous size has been proved by the discovery of the shells.

The eggs of the moa, an ancient bird of New Zealand, were very large; and those of the Aepyornis maximus were equal to about one hundred and fifty of those of the common fowl, and had a long diameter of over a foot.

Bird's nesting is allowable in the interest of science, and collections of eggs increase in value as the species decrease.

This is shown by the price brought by a single egg of the great auk, which was sold in London in 1888 for $1,100.

Only sixty-seven specimens of these eggs are known to exist, though two hundred years ago the birds were plenty.

QUEER EGGS.

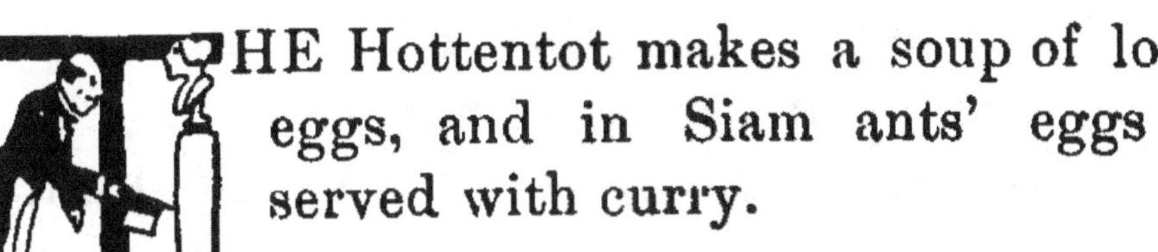THE Hottentot makes a soup of locust eggs, and in Siam ants' eggs are served with curry.

Eggs of reptiles, those of the lizard, boa constrictor, crocodile, alligator and turtle are also eaten; the latter is considered a great luxury.

Dr. Livingston, in his Explorations of the Zambezi, says of crocodiles' eggs:

"In taste they resemble hens' eggs, with perhaps a smack of custard, and would be as highly relished by whites as blacks were it not for their unsavory origin in man-eaters."

A dainty not generally known is the sea-egg; that of the sea-urchin or *strongylocentrotus.*

In this connection may be mentioned the edible birds-nests of Java and Sumatra. The sea-swallows' nests which hang on the rocks like watch-pockets.

They are about the size of a goose egg, of a thin fibrous substance like isinglass, of a slightly reddish color

It is a great labor to clean them for market. When dry they are brittle and wrinkled, and sell for twice their weight in silver.

They are served floating in a soup like lumps of jelly.

Bad eggs are so bad that they are rarely used, and disease is not likely to come from them as sometimes results from the use of the flesh of diseased animals.

The Chinese have a fondness for half-hatched eggs, and travelers have come across other people who considered eggs of extreme age as great delicacies.

SOME EGG RECIPES.

THE accompanying recipes are intended to be suggestive as well as helpful for ordinary home life.

For more elaborate preparations reference may be made to the standard French cook-books.

BOILED EGGS.

"There is always a best way of doing everything, if it be to boil an egg."

EMERSON.

Yet this which seems the simplest of all cookery, is rarely done in the best way. Usually eggs are plunged into a kettle where the water is kept rapidly boiling for three minutes; then the yolk is raw while the white is overdone.

The white will be better digested and the yolks more evenly cooked if the eggs are not boiled at all.

Either put into cold water and heat gradually, or into boiling water and remove it from the fire.

W. M. Williams, in his *Chemistry of Cooking,* says on this subject:

"Cook one in the orthodox manner by keeping it in boiling water three and a half minutes.

Then place the other in this same boiling water, but instead of keeping the saucepan over the fire, place it on the hearth and leave it there with the egg in it about ten minutes more.

A comparison of results will show that the egg that has been cooked at a temperature of more than thirty degrees below the boiling-point of water is tender and delicate, evenly so throughout, no part being hard while another part is semi-raw and slimy."

CUSTARD EGGS.

Put in cold water, and place the dish over a quick fire. When the water boils the eggs will be ready to serve.

The white will mix readily with the yolk as

in custard. Dr. Edward Smith says : " Perhaps the most agreeable form is the flaky state, in which the egg may be obtained when placed in cold water and eaten very soon after the water has been boiled."

HARD-BOILED EGGS.

Always cook for twenty minutes, then the yolk will be dry and mealy, not tough and gluey as when boiled for a shorter period. Put in cold water, that the shells may be removed easily.

STEAMED EGGS.

Cook in an ordinary steamer for five minutes, more or less, to suit the taste. They may also be broken into buttered cups and then steamed, but that is really a form of poached eggs.

For an invalid beat light, season, and steam only till well warmed through.

EGGS A LA COQUE.

Are simply eggs boiled in the usual manner, and generally eaten from the shell.

———

Eggs are often boiled at the table, but the average American cannot wait for that, and would sooner take his chances with an over or underdone egg. An egg-boiler consists of an egg-shaped cup, to contain the water which is heated by an alcohol lamp beneath; a movable frame, with rings like a caster, holds the eggs.

The freshness of eggs for boiling should be undoubted, but when one or two days old they are better than if just laid, as a part of the water will have evaporated and the white will coagulate sooner.

When dropped suddenly into boiling water egg-shells crack like glass. If a wire holder is not available roll them gently from a spoon, or put the eggs in the kettle and pour the water slowly over them.

If the shells are slightly chipped when taken from the kettle, the steam will escape and the eggs stop cooking sooner; otherwise the longer they wait the harder they grow. It is, however, best to serve them in a warm dish under a folded napkin.

How to eat a boiled egg is often a matter of discussion. Byron is said to have remarked that " the greatest trial to a woman's beauty is the ungraceful act of eating eggs."

Dean Swift tells us that the Lilliputian nation declared war against Blefuscu because its inhabitants refused to break their eggs at the end, which the Dame Fashion of Lilliput decreed was proper.

Our English cousins say " always eat a boiled egg from the shell; any other method greatly detracts from the rich flavor of this nutritious food."

This may be true, but since to do it in a civilized manner, a special set of egg-spoons is necessary, is it not better for each family to adjust the matter according to its own convenience?

POACHED EGGS.

" Egges well poched are better than roasted. They (egges) be most holesome whan they be poched."   Sir T. Elyot.

" So they be potched or rare boyled, they need no preparation or mixture."

Francis Bacon.

" A couple of poached eggs with a few, fine, dry fried collops of pure bacon, are not bad for breakfast or to begin a meal."
Sir Kenelm Digby. — *Closet of Cookery*, 1669.

Eggs cooked in this fashion are sometimes called dropped eggs, while scrambled eggs are often said to be poached.

The word poach comes from the same root as pocket, meaning literally to pierce or invade. Hence a poached egg is one where the shell is pierced and the egg taken out before boiling.

" Some outlandish bishop, not aware that he had finished his poached eggs, went on calmly sopping his bread in the water where they had been boiled."

Have ready a shallow pan nearly full of boiling salted water. A little vinegar or lemon juice and salt in the water help to harden the albumen and keep the egg in good shape. Muffin rings set in the water tend to the same results, and there are egg-poachers with perforated cups of fancy shapes.

Break the eggs singly; if the yolk breaks reserve for other uses. Stir the water briskly and slip the egg quickly into the eddy thus made, and continue to stir till the outside of the egg has hardened.

Dip the water up with a spoon and pour over the egg until a film forms over the yolk. Let the pan stand for two minutes where the water will simmer but not boil; when the white is firm drain carefully on a skimmer, and serve hot.

Poached eggs should not be cooked until hard. If rightly done, this is the most delicate way to cook eggs, as there will be none of the taste of lime sometimes noticed when they are boiled in the shell. Eggs served in this way are also attractive to the eye.

The famous Dr. Kitchener says :
• " The beauty of a Poached Egg is for the Yolk to be seen blushing through the White, which should only be just sufficiently hardened to form a transparent veil for the egg."

Eggs may also be poached in milk, soup-stock or gravy, which is afterward poured over the toast on which they are to be served.

After thus cooking, poached eggs may be served in many different ways :

1. On rounds of plain buttered toast.

2. Around a dish of minced salt fish with milk gravy.

3. With cooked spinach or asparagus.

4. On toast, first spread with any minced meat or fish warmed in gravy.

5. In stewed tomatoes; the contrasting colors giving a pretty effect.

6. On slices of ham or bacon, boiled, fried or broiled.

7. Spanish fashion, on boiled rice ; allow one tablespoonful of raw rice for each egg.

8. On top of a fish-ball place a poached egg.

9. Serve in clear soups.

10. Toast spread with cheese prepared as Welsh Rarebit, with a poached egg on top, is known as Golden Buck.

A Yorkshire rarebit is the same, with the addition of a few bits of bacon.

Poached egg received also the names of various sauces which are sometimes served with them.

WHIPPED EGGS.

Break into hot water, boil two minutes, pour off the water, beat the eggs thoroughly, season and serve on toast.

EGGS IN BALLS.

Stir the boiling water till it whirls rapidly, drop in the egg already broken into a cup, and stir the water around it until the egg is cooked. Do but one at a time.

EGG KROMESKYS AND FRITTERS.

Dip eggs already poached in a seasoned batter and fry for one minute in deep fat. The outside will be crisp and the inside soft.

Or dip the eggs in crumbs, or inclose in a crust of mashed potato, and fry or sauté in a little fat.

BAKED EGGS.

These are half-way between poaching and frying, and are also known as shirred eggs.

Œufs sur la Plat, etc. etc.

Muffin rings, fancy tin dishes, paper cases, etc., are used to cook these in, but best of all, is a shallow earthen dish, just large enough for one egg, as they are to be served in the dish in which they are cooked. The dish is buttered, the egg then broken into it, without breaking the yolk. Sprinkle with salt and pepper, and bake just long enough to set the white.

Variations.

1. Put a bit of butter or a teaspoonful of cream on top.

2. In the dish put a spoonful of gravy, sprinkle the egg with crumbs.

3. Season with a speck of nutmeg.

4. Line the dishes with grated cheese, chopped meat, parsley, or crumbs, before putting in the eggs, and turn out before serving. The Germans call these overturned eggs.

5. Cover a plate or the little dishes with a mixture of cold chopped meat and crumbs, seasoned and moistened. Make hollows for each egg and bake till they are done and the crust is crisp.

6. Swiss Eggs. Put a thin slice of cheese under each, and sprinkle with crumbs and cheese.

7. Egg Nests. Beat whites of eggs stiff, pile lightly on slices of toast, then drop the yolks which were left in the shells in a hollow in each, and bake.

FRIED EGGS.

This is one of the oldest fashions of serving eggs. In the *Piers Ploughman*, we read of "Egges yfryed with grece," among other "sundry metes."

They may be fried with ham, or bacon, in butter, olive or other oils. The cotton seed lard now in the market, is one of the best mediums for frying anything.

The frying-pan should contain hot fat enough to nearly cover the eggs. Break them simply into a cup and slip gently into the fat. Do not attempt to turn them, but dip the fat over.

Sometimes eggs are beaten, and strained through a coarse colander into hot fat, then drained and served on toast or with bacon.

Beurre Noir, or browned butter, may be served with either baked or poached eggs, but oftener with fried. Add more if necessary to that used for frying, let it brown, and add an equal quantity of vinegar. Let it boil away a little, stir in some chopped parsley and pour over the eggs.

Eggs cooked in fat are indigestible, because the high temperature of the fat — three hundred to four hundred degrees — hardens the albumen so the digestive fluids cannot penetrate it.

ROASTED EGGS.

" The vulgar boil, the learned roast an egg."
· ALEXANDER POPE.

This was probably the original way of cooking eggs, as of meats. It was the Celtic method, and Martial mentions it as common among the Romans.

People fortunate enough to live in camp have discovered anew this delightful way of serving eggs. A soft, velvet-like substance results, which cannot be obtained by any other method of cooking. Unless the shells are slightly pricked, a sudden explosion may surprise the watchers round the camp-fire.

The large ends are placed down, the whole covered with leaves, ashes and coals heaped on top, and left there for ten minutes.

Dr. King, in his *Art of Cookery*, says :
" I wish the world were thoroughly informed of two truths concerning eggs; how incomparably better roasted eggs are than boiled, and never to eat any butter with eggs in the shell."

SCRAMBLED EGGS.

By this method the white and yolk are mingled less than in omelet and more than in poaching. The result is a mottled mass of white and yellow; similar mixtures are also known as rumbled and coddled eggs.

Put in a saucepan one tablespoonful of butter for six eggs; break the eggs in, one by one, add one half cup milk and a little salt and pepper. Stir until well thickened. Serve on toast, or heap in a mound, on a hot platter. This may be prepared at the table by a chafing-dish.

Variations.

1. Use gravy or soup stock instead of milk.
2. Add one tablespoonful grated cheese or chopped parsley.

3. Use stewed tomato in place of milk; the red, white and yellow give a fine effect.

4. Travelers in the East remember with pleasure a way in which eggs are served there. It is unlike either poaching, frying, or scrambling, but resembles all. A thick pottery dish is placed over the charcoal fire to warm through, and butter, pepper and salt are placed in it. The eggs are dropped in, cooked slowly, with little stirring, and served very hot.

SOUPS.

Eggs, at first thought, have less connection with soups than with most other articles of food, but here, too, they are needed.

The Germans make sweet egg soups, something like a warm custard; their nudels or noodles require eggs for lightness.

When eggs are used to thicken soups it should be just before serving, as they require little cooking. Beat them, add a little warm soup, then strain into the whole, stirring constantly.

TO CLEAR SOUPS.

Allow the shell and white of one egg to every quart of stock. Remove all fat, add more seasoning if desired, and beat the egg thoroughly with the stock while cold. Heat gradually, stirring, to prevent the egg from settling, until it boils, then leave it to boil five to ten minutes; till a scum rises. Add a little cold water, strain carefully through a cloth and wire strainer.

Poached eggs are often served in such soups.

NOODLES.

Work flour into a beaten egg till it forms a stiff dough. Roll out very **thin,** cut in strips, and cook in the soup. Or, grate the dough, let it dry as it falls, then use in soups.

Kaiser soup.— Beat three eggs; add one cup rich, clear soup, season with salt and spice, if liked, strain into a buttered mould. Cover and steam thirty minutes, or till firm. When cold cut in slices, then in fancy shapes, and serve in clear soup.

This is also known as Savory Custard and Royale Paste.

Egg balls.— Make a paste of four yolks of hard-boiled eggs, season and moisten with raw egg. Shape in balls the size of a marble, boil or fry, and serve in soups.

Whole hard-boiled yolks are also served in soups.

OMELETS.

> " I've heard about a pleasant land
> Where omelets grow on trees."
> Tom Hood.

From the days when Sarah, Duchess of Marlborough, had to prepare the omelets to suit her husband's taste, to the time an American senator finds pleasure in his skill in the preparation of this dish, the omelet has been considered difficult of preparation.

It is told of Napoleon I., in Abbott's History, that attempting to make an omelet he failed in the cooking and exclaimed:

" I have given myself credit for more exalted talents than I possess."

Sir Henry Thompson declares the omelet " to be one of the most delicious and nutritious products of culinary art, with the further merit that it can be more rapidly prepared than any other dish."

The name derived from the French words, *œufs mêlés* — eggs mingled — shows the nationality of the dish.

The omelet is a combination of eggs and milk, well seasoned and cooked in butter; to it may be added small quantities of meat, fish, vegetables, or fruit; of little value by themselves, but which increase its substance and savoriness.

These various materials which give special names to omelets are usually cooked separately, and are spread over or around the omelet after cooking, and just before serving.

A Soufflée (literally puffed up) is an omelet usually baked, and to which some fruit or jelly is added.

A Fondu (meaning something poured) is a sort of omelet in which cheese is used for flavoring.

There are really but two ways of making omelet; the French omelet, when the yolks and whites of the eggs are beaten together — the Puffy omelet when they are beaten separately.

It is better to cook several small omelets than one large one, because of danger of burning and trouble in turning. If for a side dish, one egg for each person will be sufficient, and two or three eggs are all that should be cooked at once.

If the eggs be separated, beat the yolks till lighter colored, and the whites till stiff and dry. Many cooks prefer to use more yolks than whites in their omelets.

When yolks and whites are together, too much beating is said to make the omelet watery; but the parts must be well mingled, not show as in scrambled eggs.

The beating must be continued until the omelet is put in the pan, or the air which has been beaten in will escape.

Some cooks use eggs alone, but the omelet will be more creamy if milk be used in the proportion of one tablespoonful to each egg. Water, soup-stock or gravy may be substituted for the milk.

As flour and cornstarch require more cooking than egg, they should not be used unless previously cooked in the milk. Stale bread-crumbs where the starch has already been cooked is a better thickening if any be desired.

Authorities differ as to seasoning an omelet before or after cooking; some claim that salt makes it flabby if added before.

A speck of salt and pepper may be safely used at first and more added later.

Beat the eggs, add the milk — if the whites are beaten separately, fold lightly into yolks and milk — salt and pepper, and pour at once into the pan in which is one teaspoonful of hot butter.

Cooked in a large, cold pan over a slow fire a leathery mass results, unworthy the name of omelet.

A clear fire, a smooth pan, clean, dry and hot, are essential. To insure perfect smoothness some cooks recommend heating a little fat in the pan, then pouring it out and wiping the pan dry before putting in the butter for the omelet. Others say never use an omelet pan for anything else.

Special pans are manufactured for this purpose, but any small, smooth pan will do.

If a large pan must be used it should be so tipped and held that the omelet may cook upon one side instead of spreading thinly over the whole pan.

Use only enough butter to keep from sticking.

The albumen of the eggs begins to harden at once on the edges, and this part may be drawn to one side with a fork, or a knife may be run under the center, raising the cooked portion and giving the remainder a chance to run underneath.

The pan should be gently shaken meantime to prevent the omelet from adhering anywhere.

If necessary the top may be hardened by placing the pan in a hot oven for one minute.

As soon as all is firm — in three to five minutes — roll over and over or spread with the cooked meat or vegetables, and slipping a knife under fold one side upon the other. Then turn upside down on a warm platter and serve immediately.

Better the family wait for the omelet than the omelet wait for the family.

Omelets may also be baked in a buttered pudding dish.

To an omelet of two to four eggs, any of the following ingredients may be added, either before or after cooking, in the proportion of from one to three tablespoonfuls.

Anchovy. — The prepared paste is spread thinly over the omelet before folding.

Apple. — The apples are cooked, sifted, sweetened, spiced; one half cupful is then spread over the omelet, or the eggs are beaten with it and the mixture is baked.

Asparagus. — Fold in the tips of cooked asparagus.

Bacon. — Cut cooked bacon in strips or dice and mix with the eggs before frying.

Bread. — Soak one half cup of crumbs in one half cup of milk, beat with two eggs, fry or bake.

Caviare. — Use like anchovy.

Cauliflower. — Like asparagus.

Celery. — Cook and use in the same fashion.

Cheese. — Parmesan or Gruyère are best; any dry cheese may be grated or chopped and one to three tablespoonfuls added to the omelet before or after cooking.

Chicken. — May be chopped or cut in small pieces.

Clams. — Should be chopped.

Corn. — Sweet corn pulp or canned corn chopped fine, can be added before cooking the omelet.

Creamy Omelet. — Cook together one teaspoonful each of flour or butter, gradually add one half cup of milk, and when partly cool add beaten yolks of two eggs, seasoning, and then the stiff whites. Fry or bake.

Fish. — One half cup of minced fish, salt or fresh; warm in milk or cream sauce; serve around the omelet.

Garlic. — Rub the frying pan with the garlic before putting in the omelet.

Ham. — Chop cold-boiled, broiled or fried ham very fine; sprinkle over the omelet before *it is* quite done.

Herbs. — For seasoning use a speck of sweet herbs, powdered thyme, marjoram, etc.

Indian. — One tablespoonful of cooked rice and one teaspoonful of curry mixed to a paste with cream and put inside the omelet.

Italian. — One tablespoonful of macaroni cooked and cut in small pieces, one teaspoonful of grated cheese, one tablespoonful of strained tomato. Heat, season with salt, cayenne and nutmeg and roll in the omelet.

Jelly. — Before folding spread with one tablespoonful of jelly. Dust the outside with powdered sugar.

Kidney. — Cook the kidneys, slice and season; when the omelet is ready fold them inside it.

Lobster. — Cut small or chop, fold in or serve around the omelet to get the effect of the contrasting colors.

Macaroni. — Into the raw omelet stir two tablespoonfuls of cooked macaroni; bake or fry as usual.

Macedoine. — In the ordinary omelet fold a mixture of carrot, peas, beans, beets or turnips cut small, cooked, seasoned and warmed in butter or cream sauce.

Onion. — Use a pan in which an onion has been fried. If more flavor is wanted garnish with the fried onion.

Oyster. — Add chopped or whole oysters to the omelet before it is cooked, or parboil and drain them and add just before folding.

Parsley. — Put one tablespoonful of chopped parsley in before cooking.

Peach. — Rub three ripe peaches through a sieve, sweeten, add the yolks of three eggs, then the stiff whites and bake.

Peas. — Use green peas as a garnish around the omelet.

Potato. — Fry the potatoes, and serve in and around the omelet. Or, mix one half cup of mashed potato with three beaten eggs. Bake or fry.

Preserves. — Use any preserve, like jelly omelet.

Raspberry. — Make like Peach Omelet, using one cup of raspberry pulp.

Salmon. — Add two tablespoonfuls of minced salmon before or after cooking.

Sardine. — Like salmon, and garnish with whole sardines.

Sausage. — Add one tablespoonful of crumbled sausage before cooking, and garnish with whole ones.

Strawberry. — Fold in mashed strawberries, garnish with whole ones and sprinkle with powdered sugar.

Shrimp. — Place picked shrimps in the center, garnish with whole ones.

Sorrel. — Boil and sift the sorrel, place in small mounds around or fold inside the omelet.

Soufflé. — T. J. Murrey, in *Puddings and Dainty Desserts*, says : " Beat separately the whites of four and the yolks of two eggs ; whisk the whites into the yolks; add a tablespoonful of sugar and a few drops of vanilla extract, turn it out on a shallow tin or plate, and bake ten or twelve minutes. Serve immediately on the dish in which it was baked."

The secret is to beat the eggs thoroughly, and serve the moment it is taken from the oven.

Spinach. — Before cooking the omelet, add one tablespoonful of boiled and sifted spinach.

Sweetbread. — Cook the sweetbread, and prepare like kidneys.

Tomato. — Use strained tomato in place of milk. Garnish with sliced tomatoes.

Tongue. — Fold in boiled tongue chopped fine.

Traveler's Omelet. — Spread with chopped meat, roll like a jelly cake, cut in slices and put in sandwiches.

Truffles. — Like mushrooms.

Vermicelli. — Like macaroni.

WAYS OF SERVING HARD-BOILED EGGS.

There are many side dishes, of which hard-boiled eggs are the foundation, suitable for breakfast and lunch.

Such different names have been applied to dishes which may only differ in a single minor ingredient, that no names are given here.

Any fruit, vegetable, meat or fish that may be used with eggs for omelets can be combined with hard-boiled egg to produce quite a different effect.

For convenience we will first consider how to serve the eggs in their original shape.

The eggs are to be boiled twenty minutes; those left from breakfast can be re-cooked. Then, if covered at once with cold water, sudden contraction will make the shell come off easily when broken.

STUFFED EGGS.

Cut in halves, cross or lengthwise, without breaking the whites, scoop out the yolks and rub them to a paste. Moisten with melted butter, olive oil, gravy, cream sauce, stock or raw egg. Of minced meat, fish, cheese, truffles or mushrooms, etc., add as much as there is of the egg paste. Season highly with salt, pepper, mustard, onion or curry, etc. Mix all well together. Fill the whites again and press together.

The whites may be dug out to hold still more of the force-meat. If there is any of it left the eggs may be covered, rolled in raw egg and crumbs and fried. Or the force-meat may be piled in the center of a dish and the eggs arranged upon it; or it can be made into little balls to serve with the eggs.

Stuffed eggs are served hot with various sauces, or cold with lettuce and dressing as a salad.

For picnics twist each egg in a fringed square of white tissue paper.

SCOTCH EGGS.

Cook together one third cup of milk and one third cup of stale crumbs, add one cup of lean ham chopped fine, and one raw beaten egg; mix well. Cover whole or stuffed hard-boiled eggs with the mixture.

Fry them, cut in quarters or slices, and serve cold for lunch or picnics.

EGG DUMPLINGS.

(Old Recipe.) Wrap hard-boiled eggs in puff paste and fry them.

NUREMBERG EGGS.

(German Recipe.) Shell hard-boiled eggs, dip in batter, fry brown in butter. Dip again, and fry again, and so on till it becomes a large ball.   Serve with sauce.

EGG BASKETS.

Cut a slice from each end of an egg, then cut in halves crosswise.   Prepare the yolks as for stuffed eggs.   Fill the whites again even full, and place a cover of pickled beet on top; or, make balls of the force-meat, put in the baskets, and stick a sprig of parsley in the top. Serve like stuffed eggs.

HARD-BOILED EGGS SLICED OR CHOPPED.

1. *Scalloped Eggs (Eggs Au Gratin).* — Slice six or eight hard-boiled eggs, put in a pudding-dish with one pint of sauce made with cream or soup-stock, and seasoned with salt, pepper and parsley.   One or two tablespoonfuls of grated cheese is often put in the sauce.   Sprinkle with buttered crumbs and brown in the oven.

2. Instead of cheese use chopped onion.

3. Put sliced eggs and oysters in alternate layers, and cover with plain cream sauce.

4. Add a dash of curry to the sauce and combine with rice already cooked.

5. Slice the eggs, dip each piece in egg and crumbs and fry.

6. Warm chopped eggs in a rich sauce; serve in puff paste shells.

7. *Lyonnaise.* — Fry a chopped onion in butter, add whites of eggs chopped fine; when hot put on a platter and garnish with the yolks.

8. To one pint of cream sauce add the chopped whites of six eggs; season with salt and pepper, pour over slices of toast. Rub the hard yolks through a strainer over the top.

9. *Sandwiches.* — Chop, butter and season the eggs, and while still warm spread slices of bread with the mixture and press them together.

GARNISHES.

Golden Rain. — The yolk of hard-boiled eggs rubbed through a strainer, and left just as it falls over salads or fish or meat, gives a pleasing effect.

Egg Daisies. — Cut the white of hard-boiled eggs in strips and arrange like the daisy petals on the edges of a platter, and place a little mound of the sifted yolk for the center.

EGGS FOR INVALIDS.

A well-known physician says that many lives are lost by starvation, owing to an over-estimate of the nutritive value of beef-tea and meat juices, but that "There is no good substitute for milk and eggs."

An English physician adds this word: "In cases of depression, where disordered working of the brain tends to exhaust the strength, I rely more and more on milk and eggs made into liquid custards. Sixteen eggs daily are given with good results."

The egg has been said to be " A maximum of nutrition requiring a minimum of digestive force."

The white of the egg is constipating in effect, the yolk laxative; the latter is considered helpful in jaundice and similar disorders on account of the oil it contains, while the white is useful in diseases opposite in nature.

The egg is now considered valuable in typhus and typhoid fevers, dysentery and similar disorders. Taken raw it forms a slight coating over the stomach and other organs, and by its soothing qualities reduces inflammation. On the same principle the white of the egg beaten with a little sugar and water has been recommended for children with irritable stomachs.

Nothing will sooner relieve a feeling of exhaustion than a raw egg beaten in a glass of milk, and sweetened and seasoned to the taste. Such a drink furnishes more real energy than tea or alcoholic beverages, and without their evil effects ; many a tired woman would be better for it.

Eggs may also be served in tea, coffee, lemonade or hot broth in the same fashion.

Physicians object to excessive beating of eggs for invalids, since if much air be mingled in them it may give rise to wind in the stomach; but if slightly beaten the solidity of the egg being broken the gastric juice can work upon it more freely.

Any person who cannot take milk may substitute coffee, tea or broth.

The following drinks are suitable for invalids or tired persons who call themselves well.

EGGNOG PLAIN.

Beat white and yolk together or separately, sweeten and flavor to the taste. Add one half to one cup cold or warm milk or boiling water.

Either white or yolk alone will often be more acceptable and digest sooner than if taken together. Eggs become difficult of digestion in proportion as they lose their freshness.

EGG MILK.

(*Lait de Poule.*) Beat a fresh egg with a speck of salt, pour into one pint of boiling milk, stirring all the time, and take hot.

EGG BROTH.

Stir a beaten egg into one cup of hot meat broth; drink while warm.

EGG COFFEE.

Beat one yolk with one teaspoonful of sugar, pour on one cup of boiling coffee, stirring as it thickens. Add cream if preferred, but eggs make a very good substitute for milk or cream whenever it cannot be obtained.

Egg Tea is made in the same way.

CUSTARDS.

Use four to six eggs to one quart of milk, sweeten and flavor to taste.

The eggs require only so much beating as

will break up the particles of the egg that it may readily mix with the milk.

The best cooks prefer to use yolks only in making custards; in that case double the number of eggs and use the whites for other things.

It is an easy matter to mix custards, but they are often spoiled by over cooking.

Custards will cook where water would not boil. If the applied heat be greater than that of boiling water, or be too long continued, the solid and liquid constituents of the eggs and milk will separate — the custard wheys or curdles, and becomes unpalatable and indigestible.

SHAKER FISH AND EGG.

Heat in a common saucepan one pint of new milk, or thin cream if you have it. Season with salt, and let it simmer for a few minutes. Remove a portion of this gravy into another vessel and dissolve therein a small piece of butter. Into the saucepan slice a layer of boiled potatoes, making the slices say three eighths of an inch thick; to this add a little salt codfish, boiled and picked very fine, then a layer of boiled eggs, each egg cut in four or five slices. Alternate with another layer of potato, fish and egg, until the desired quantity is obtained. Now pour on the reserved gravy and cover over for a few minutes, or until ready to place upon the table. When dished up, place upon the top some of the sliced eggs. The eggs should be boiled six minutes, and then immediately immersed in cold water. This prevents them from becoming too hard, and also toughens the shell, thus rendering it more easily removed. For four persons, about eight eggs and eight medium-sized potatoes are needed. This quantity will require of salt fish, about three tablespoonfuls, when nicely prepared. This is really a delectable dish.

EGG APPLES.

" Boil the eggs hard. Remove the shells one by one, while they are under the water; press both ends softly between the first finger and thumb till it assumes the shape of an apple. Color each slightly with red, or make little spots to simulate the appearance of an apple.

If real apple leaves or stems cannot be obtained, get some other and decorate with them.

Pile them in a dainty dish and place it on the table and it will make a pretty display of untimely apples, pleasing to the eyes, and satisfying to the taste."

Miss Kin Kato, of Japan.

BEATING EGGS.

WHILE many recipes might appropriately be given here for foods where egg is the most important ingredient, lack of space prevents; but these points should be remembered in all doughs made light by eggs.

The peculiar viscidity of albumen makes the egg an important factor in cookery. If carefully beaten, it catches and holds for a time a large quantity of air, and if cooked at once doughs are made light.

The pound and sponge cakes and batter puddings of our grandmothers had nothing but eggs to give them the delicate lightness rarely seen now. From the higher price of eggs and a lack of knowledge about their use, baking powders have largely superseded them, and our food and stomachs have suffered in proportion.

There are two objects in beating eggs; to

mingle the two parts of the egg, and to incorporate air with it.

For custards, etc., the first is all that is required. For cakes more beating is necessary to accomplish the latter.

A variety of beaters are in the market, all doing the work in a more or less perfect way. But many of the best cooks, except for a large quantity of eggs, prefer a knife or fork or simple whip to the more elaborate machines.

To gain the greatest possible amount of air, yolks and whites must be separated.

The snowy appearance of the beaten white is caused by the mixture of air and probably also by a slight evaporation of water, since it becomes frothy sooner in a draught of air. The oil, which the yolk contains, makes it lighter than the white, as is shown by its position in the shell, and when the two parts are beaten together it acts like oil on troubled waters, making it impossible for the air to get in or for any water to pass off.

Cold eggs beat quicker than those that have been in a warm place. A little salt, or cream of tartar, either of which stiffen albumen, help the beating process. Beat slowly at first, but more rapidly at the end.

For cakes and some omelets, the whites require to be beaten very dry even after successfully trying the old test of turning the bowl upside down. Yet there is such a thing as beating eggs too much.

Yolks should be beaten till they become lighter colored and thicken. Never leave beaten eggs to stand, as all the air will escape.

Beaten whites must be folded very carefully into the other ingredients after they are well mixed, and the dough baked at once.

Beaten eggs are used to glaze pastry. Also for covering croquettes, etc., before frying, since the albumen hardens quickly and the fats cannot then penetrate. If not beaten enough it will slip off, leaving bare patches; if too much beaten it will be frothy and not adhere on that account.

A spoonful of water or milk may be added to each egg for economy. For oysters, etc., season the egg with salt and pepper; for sweet croquettes use a speck of sugar.

EGGS IN CHINA.

MR. FRANK G. CARPENTER, a recent traveler in China, says :

The Chinese are very fond of eggs, but they never eat them soft-boiled, and they believe that an egg grows better with age. Preserved eggs are one of the dainties of China, and it takes forty days to pickle them. The eggs are covered with a mixture of tea-leaves, lime, salt and wood-ashes, made into a paste, and are then packed away in wood-ashes, which all over China are sold to the egg-packers for this purpose. The older an egg grows after packing the better it is supposed to be. There are methods of pickling which turn the eggs as black as jet. In some cases they are steeped in water in which the leaves of fir or cedar-trees have been boiled. The Chinese also pickle eggs in salt water, and they regard these salted eggs as good for medicinal purposes. They have certain festivals at which they give presents of hard-boiled, dyed eggs, and when a child is born the family and friends celebrate the event by a feast of dyed eggs. All told, the egg-industry of China gives employment to many thousand people, and forms one of the important specialties of this very busy nation.

———

It is one of the triumphs of Chinese cookery to pierce and blow the eggs and re-fill them with vari-colored and vari-flavored custards and jellies. The apertures are sealed, and the outside of the shells painted like a nightmare, with dragons, griffins, etc.

MISCELLANEOUS.

IF raw yolks of eggs are put in a churn, just before the butter comes, their color will be imparted to the butter.

Shells burned in the oven and then placed on pantry shelves are said to repel vermin.

Broken in bits, with cold water and a little soda, the shells, with their jagged edges, will clean glass bottles.

Shells broken only at one end are convenient molds for blanc-mange and jellies.

Old-time receipt books mention egg-shells as dishes to set in the ashes, in which to melt salves and ointments.

One Swedish dish is an omelet of cheese, butter, milk and egg, cooked in the dish in which it is to be served.

An Italian cook serves perfumed eggs where a faint but delicious flavor of violets, roses, etc., is imparted by rubbing the dish with the extract.

"Stir them with steady hand and conscience
          pricking,
To see the untimely end of ten fine chicken."

" The egg is to the kitchen what the articles are in discourse; that is to say, a necessity so indispensable that the most skillful must renounce his art if the use of it was forbidden him."
Almanach des Gourmands.— Paris, 1804.

" The relation of a hen to a dozen fair, white, pure eggs, and the relation of those eggs to puddings and custards, and the twenty-five cents which they can have for the asking, make even an ungainly hen, like many heroines in novels, not beautiful but interesting."
GAIL HAMILTON.
A Prose Henriade, Atlantic Monthly, June, '65.

" Where would be the piquant salads, golden

sponge cake, delicate custards and frozen creams and puddings and the thousand and one things we owe to the egg?"

H. W. BEECHER.

Philadelphia, according to *The Record*, eats in the course of the year 200,000,000 eggs, of which seven eighths come from Iowa, Kansas, Minnesota and Nebraska, packed in refrigerator cars holding 144,000 each.

In the ordinances of fares to be served to the King's Highness and the Queen's Grace as made at Eltham in the seventeenth year of King Henry VIII., butter and eggs appear in the second course on both Flesh and Fish Days. "The ordinary prices for all kinds of poultry stuff to be served by the aforesaid William Gurley" as decreed in these ordinances: "For eggs from Shrovetide till Michaelmas, the hundred, 14d.   For eggs from Michaelmas till Shrovetide, the hundred, 20d."

THE STORK.

A bird of great antiquity and dignity is the stork; it was known to the writers of the Bible, and was a favorite with Æsop.

It might well have been chosen as an Easter emblem; for there is a Swedish legend that it fluttered around the cross of Christ, crying: " Stykê, Stykê, Strengthen ye, Strengthen ye," and thus it lost its voice and received its name.

In Holland it is regarded with veneration, and happy is the house upon whose roof it makes the nest for its pale, yellow eggs. The Dutch name for the stork can be traced to an old word, meaning the bringer of good.

THE HARE'S EGGS.

" Hare, hare, good little hare, lay plenty of eggs for us on Easter Day," sing the German children.

The reason for the popular idea that at Easter time the hare becomes an oviparous animal seems, at first, almost unaccountable.

German authors, however, tell us that the hare, because of its fruitfulness, was sacred to Ostara, the goddess of spring and of love; and that this explains the belief that Easter eggs were produced by hares rather than by hens.

In the folk-lore of many savage tribes the hare is a type of the moon, since, because of its short upper eyelid, it always sleeps with its eyes open.

The Aztecs saw a hare rather than a man in the moon.

The Egyptians often represented Osiris as a beautiful hare. Hares may have drawn the chariot of Ostara as the cats drew that of Freya.

Many Indian races worship the dawn as a mystical hare. The leaping hare was considered an emblem of spring-time or the approach of day, by nearly all races.

INDEX.